Chocolate

Chocolate

Joanna Farrow

hamlyn

Published in the UK in 1996
by Hamlyn, a division of Octopus Publishing Group Ltd
2–4 Heron Quays, London E14 4JP

This edition published 2001

ISBN 0 600 60575 2

Printed in China

NOTES

Both metric and imperial measurements have been given
in all recipes. Use one set of measurements only and not a
mixture of both.

Standard level spoon measurements are used in all recipes.
1 tablespoon = one 15 ml spoon
1 teaspoon = one 5 ml spoon

Eggs should be medium unless otherwise stated.

Milk should be full fat unless otherwise stated.

Ovens should be preheated to the specified temperature – if
using a fan-assisted oven, follow the manufacturer's instructions
for adjusting the time and the temperature.

Contents

Introduction

The willpower of even the most health-conscious eaters among us seems to crumble at the mere mention of chocolate. Its rich colour, unique texture, tempting aroma and delicious flavour have, since its discovery centuries ago, provided one of the most irresistible, ever-fashionable foods.

There is an increasingly wide choice of different types of chocolate available. Careful selection of the right one will take you halfway to culinary success.

PLAIN CHOCOLATE

This is generally the best chocolate to use for cooking, although the quality can vary considerably. Choose a chocolate that contains a high proportion of 'cocoa solids'. This can vary from anywhere between 30 to 70 per cent, and should be specified on the wrapping. Although chocolate containing a higher proportion of cocoa solids will be more expensive, it will give a stronger and smoother flavour. For dipped chocolate and Easter eggs, choose a chocolate containing at least 70 per cent cocoa solids.

MILK CHOCOLATE

This contains between 15 and 30 per cent cocoa solids and has plenty of additional cream and sugar. It has a less intense chocolate flavour but it is useful

for contrasting decorations. Chopped chunks add a delicious creamy bite to cakes and biscuits.

WHITE CHOCOLATE

This gets its flavour from 'cocoa butter', which is extracted during the chocolate processing. It is high in fat and sugar and is more likely to burn when melting. Luxury brands of white chocolate will give a richer, less sugary flavouring.

CHOCOLATE-FLAVOURED CAKE COVERING

This is a cheap imitation chocolate sold widely in supermarkets. It is made from sugar, vegetable oil, cocoa and flavourings and is best avoided in chocolate cookery. A little can be added to the chocolate when melting for caraque or

chocolate shavings (see page 7), as its high fat content makes the chocolate easier to work with, without impairing the actual flavour.

COCOA POWDER

This is another product of chocolate processing and has a strong bitter flavour. It is useful in cakes and cookies and in some desserts and puddings to accentuate the flavour of the chocolate. Drinking chocolate powder, used for hot milk drinks, is not the same thing and is not a substitute for cocoa powder.

MELTING CHOCOLATE

Break plain, milk or white chocolate into even-sized pieces and put in a heatproof bowl. Place the bowl over a saucepan containing a little gently simmering water, and leave until melted. (Make sure that the base of the bowl is not in contact with the water or the chocolate will overheat; make sure, too, that the water does not boil away.)

Gently stir the chocolate and leave it over the water for a little longer if any lumps remain. Remove from the heat, making sure that droplets of water on the bowl do not come into contact with the chocolate. (This solidifies the texture of the chocolate, making it difficult to use for decorative purposes.)

Chocolate Melted in the Microwave

Break plain, milk or white chocolate into pieces and put in a bowl (not metal). The melting times will vary according to the amount of chocolate being melted, type of bowl and temperature of the chocolate. As a guide, allow about 2 minutes on HIGH for 125 g/4 oz plain chocolate, and 2–3 minutes on MEDIUM for milk and white chocolate which have a greater tendency to burn. Let the chocolate stand for 2 minutes after microwaving, heating it for a little longer if any lumps still remain after standing.

Melting Chocolate for Decorating

The success of chocolate confectionery and Easter eggs depends largely on accurate melting. If chocolate is under- or overheated, the results will be dull and a whitish 'bloom' or discoloration may develop. Rest a chocolate thermometer (available from cake decorating specialists and kitchenware stores) in the bowl once the chocolate has just melted. For plain chocolate, the temperature should reach 46–49°C (115–120°F). For milk and white chocolate, the temperature should reach 43°C (110°F).

CHOCOLATE DECORATIONS

These decorations can make the perfect finishing touch for your special chocolate desserts and gâteaux. They can be made up to two weeks in advance and stored in an airtight container in a cool place.

If the chocolate is brittle and crumbles when you attempt to make chocolate curls, caraque or shavings, it may be too cold. If this is so, leave it for a while at room temperature to soften slightly.

Chocolate Leaves

Clean your chosen leaves, such as bay, mint or rose. Melt 50 g/2 oz plain, milk or white chocolate (this will cover about 15 leaves). Using a paintbrush, thickly coat the undersides of the leaves, taking the chocolate almost to the edges of the leaves. Leave to set on a baking tray lined with greaseproof paper. Once the chocolate is set, carefully peel away the leaves from the chocolate.

Chocolate Caraque

Melt 150 g/5 oz plain, milk or white chocolate with 25 g/1 oz plain, milk or white chocolate-flavoured cake covering, and spread on to a marble slab or a clean, smooth surface. When just set, draw a fine-bladed knife across the chocolate at an angle of 45°.

Chocolate Curls

Spread the chocolate on to the surface. When just set, push a clean wallpaper scraper across the surface to make the curls. Mini-curls can be made by using a narrower scraper.

Quick Chocolate Curls

Allow a large bar of plain, milk or white chocolate to soften in a warm room. Using a vegetable peeler, shave off curls.

Chocolate Shavings

Thoroughly wash and dry a 250 g/8 oz margarine tub or similar-sized container. Melt 300 g/10 oz plain or white chocolate with 50 g/2 oz plain or white chocolate-flavoured cake covering. Turn into the tub and leave until set but not hard. Press the chocolate out of the tub. Holding the slab of chocolate in one hand with kitchen paper (to prevent the heat of your hands melting the chocolate), pare off thin shavings with a knife.

Double Chocolate Shavings

Melt 150 g/5 oz white chocolate with 25 g/1 oz white chocolate flavoured cake covering and turn into the tub as above. Melt 150 g/5 oz plain or milk chocolate with 25 g/1 oz plain or milk chocolate-flavoured cake covering and spoon over the white chocolate. Set and shape the chocolate as above.

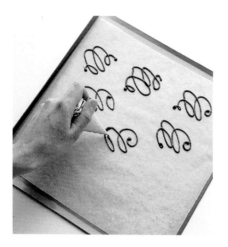

PIPED CHOCOLATE SHAPES

Line a tray with non-stick greaseproof paper. Melt a little plain or white chocolate and place in a paper piping bag. Snip off the merest tip. Pipe simple decorative motifs on to the paper. Leave to set, then peel the paper away from the chocolate.

CHOCOLATE TWISTS

Cut 8 strips out of acetate, each measuring 12 x 4 cm/5 x 1½ inches. Melt 50 g/2 oz plain or white chocolate. Spread a little down each strip to within 5 mm/¼ inch of the edges. Twist each strip so that the chocolate is on the inside and

tape the ends down on to a sturdy surface until the chocolate is set hard. Carefully lift the strips and peel away the acetate.

MODELLING PASTE RIBBONS

Thinly roll a little Chocolate Modelling Paste (see page 9) on a surface dusted lightly with cocoa powder. Cut into strips, 10–12 cm/4–5 inches long and 1.5 cm–2.5 cm/¾–1 inch wide. Arrange on a cake, lifting them at intervals to shape into ribbony waves. Bows can be shaped by bending strips into loops and arranging them in a cluster on a cake. (If they start to collapse once shaped, prop them up with crumpled greaseproof paper and store until hardened.)

MODELLING PASTE ROSES

Thinly roll a little Chocolate Modelling Paste (see page 9) on a surface dusted lightly with cocoa powder and then cut out a 15 x 4 cm/6 x 1½ inch rectangle. Fold the rectangle in half lengthways and then cut off the ends at a diagonal so that they taper to a point at the folded side. Roll up each chocolate strip, gathering it in slightly at intervals so that it resembles a simple rose.

BASIC RECIPES

GLOSSY CHOCOLATE SAUCE

Use this sauce to pour over hot puddings, profiteroles, ice cream, hot or cold crêpes and soufflés.

- 125 g/4 oz caster sugar
- 125 ml/4 fl oz cold water
- 175 g/6 oz plain chocolate, broken into pieces
- 25 g/1 oz unsalted butter
- 2 tablespoons brandy (optional)

1 Heat the sugar and water in a small heavy-based saucepan until the sugar has dissolved. Bring to the boil and boil for 1 minute.

2 Remove from the heat and stir in the chocolate and butter. Stir until dissolved, then add the brandy, if using.

ALMOND PRALINE

This is used in making chocolate confectionery and is often mixed with thick whipped cream as a delicious filling for chocolate cakes.

- 50 g/2 oz caster sugar
- 4 tablespoons cold water
- 50 g/2 oz blanched almonds, toasted

1 Lightly oil a baking sheet. Heat the sugar and water in a small heavy-based saucepan until the sugar dissolves.

2 Bring to the boil and boil until the sugar turns golden. Stir in the almonds and immediately turn out on to the oiled baking sheet.

3 Leave until brittle. Place in a double thickness polythene bag and beat with a rolling pin until finely crushed.

CHOCOLATE MODELLING PASTE

The putty-like texture of this chocolate paste makes it perfect for moulding into a variety of chocolate decorations, or for loosely draping over or around the sides of cakes (see Chocolate Truffle Gâteau on page 47). Store the paste for up to two weeks in the refrigerator.

For decorative ideas, see previous page.

- 125 g/4 oz plain or white chocolate, broken into pieces
- 2 tablespoons golden syrup or liquid glucose

1 Put the chocolate in a heatproof bowl over a saucepan of simmering water and leave until melted. Stir lightly to check that there are no lumps.
2 Remove from the heat and beat in the golden syrup or liquid glucose until the mixture forms a paste which leaves the sides of the bowl.
3 Transfer to a polythene bag and chill for about 30 minutes until firm. (If it becomes too hard to work with, leave at room temperature for a while or microwave briefly.)

CHOCOLATE GANACHE

Ganache is a mixture of chocolate and cream, used as a filling or covering for cakes. It can be swirled over cakes or gâteaux or left to thicken until sufficiently firm to pipe decoratively. If liked, a dash of brandy-, rum- or orange-flavoured liqueur can be added with the chocolate.

- 175 ml/6 fl oz double cream
- 175 g/6 oz plain chocolate, broken into pieces

1 Bring the cream just to the boil in a small saucepan. Remove from the heat and add the chocolate.
2 Stir gently until the chocolate has melted. Transfer to a bowl.
3 Leave the mixture to cool slightly, then whisk until thickened.

EQUIPMENT

DOUBLE SAUCEPAN

The most basic requirement for chocolate cookery is a suitable container for melting chocolate. This can be either a double saucepan (a small pan which sits inside a larger one) or a heatproof bowl which rests over a saucepan so that the steam cannot escape from the saucepan. The base of the bowl should be well above the base of the pan.

MARBLE SLAB

Useful, though not essential, a marble slab is perfect for setting chocolate for caraque or curls. Because of its smooth, cool surface, it is also a good surface on which to make piped and moulded chocolate decorations.

CHOCOLATE THERMOMETER

Used to ensure that chocolate is heated to the correct temperature. The thermometer is only needed for very decorative work, such as Easter eggs and chocolate confectionery, when you want to ensure a really glossy finish.

PALETTE KNIFE

Useful for spreading chocolate mixtures attractively on to cakes, or for spreading chocolate on to paper or other surfaces for making decorations.

DIPPING FORK

A long, thin-pronged fork for dipping chocolate confectionery. Cocktail sticks, which support the sweet while the excess chocolate drips back into the bowl, make a good substitute.

PIPING BAGS AND NOZZLES

Greaseproof paper piping bags are much cleaner and easier to use for chocolate work than nylon ones and are frequently used for chocolate decorations. You can either cut off 1 cm/½ inch from the tip of the piping bag and fit a metal piping nozzle, or snip off the merest tip for line piping. For convenience, make up several bags at a time (see below).

TO MAKE A GREASEPROOF PAPER PIPING BAG

Halve a 20 cm/8 inch square of greaseproof paper diagonally. With the longest side away from you, fold the right-hand point over to the point nearest you, forming a cone. Fold the left-hand point over the cone so that all four points meet. Fold the points over several times to secure. Make a few bags at the same time.

Hot Puddings

Chocolate and Spiced Apple Strudel

FILLING:

1 kg/2 lb cooking apples

2 tablespoons lemon juice

50 g/2 oz unsalted butter

50 g/2 oz breadcrumbs

1 teaspoon ground mixed spice

50 g/2 oz demerara sugar

50 g/2 oz sultanas

50 g/2 oz walnut pieces

125 g/4 oz plain chocolate, chopped

TO FINISH:

6 sheets filo pastry

50 g/2 oz unsalted butter, melted

icing sugar, for dusting

clotted or whipped cream, to serve

1 Lightly grease a large baking sheet with slightly raised sides. Peel, core and slice the apples and put in a bowl of water with the lemon juice to prevent discoloration.

2 Melt the butter in a frying pan and fry the breadcrumbs for about 3 minutes until golden. Drain the apples and add to the pan with the remaining filling ingredients.

3 Lay one sheet of filo pastry on the work surface and brush with a little of the butter. Cover with another sheet and brush with more butter. Add a third sheet and spoon half the filling down the centre of the pastry to within 2.5 cm/1 inch of the edges.

4 Fold the two short ends over the filling, then roll up the pastry like a Swiss roll, starting from a long side. Transfer to the baking sheet with the join underneath.

5 Use the remaining pastry, filling and butter to make a second strudel. Bake in a pre-heated oven, 190°C (375°F), Gas Mark 5, for about 30 minutes until golden. Cool slightly, dust with icing sugar and serve sliced with clotted or whipped cream.

Serves 8

Preparation time: 25 minutes

Cooking time: about 30 minutes

Oven temperature: 190°C (375°F), Gas Mark 5

Chocolate Puddle Pudding

This delicious oven-baked pudding separates while baking to produce a gooey chocolate sauce under a light, spongy crust. Serve it hot, well dusted with cocoa powder and with plenty of whipped cream.

- 250 g/8 oz plain chocolate, broken into pieces
- 300 ml/½ pint milk
- 2 tablespoons brandy (optional)
- 50 g/2 oz unsalted butter, softened
- 150 g/5 oz caster sugar
- 2 eggs, separated
- 25 g/1 oz self-raising flour
- 25 g/1 oz cocoa powder
- cocoa powder, for dusting

1 Put the chocolate in a small saucepan with the milk and heat gently until the chocolate has melted. Stir in the brandy, if using.

2 Beat together the butter and sugar until pale and creamy. Gradually beat in the egg yolks, flour, cocoa and melted chocolate mixture.

3 Whisk the egg whites in a separate bowl until they hold their shape. Using a large metal spoon, fold a quarter of the egg whites into the chocolate mixture, then fold in the rest of the egg whites.

4 Turn into a 1.5 litre/2½ pint pie dish and place the dish in a roasting tin. Pour a 2.5 cm/1 inch depth of boiling water into the tin. Bake in a preheated oven, 180°C (350°F), Gas Mark 4, for about 35 minutes until a crust has formed.

5 Dust generously with cocoa powder and serve hot with whipped cream.

Serves 5–6
Preparation time: 20 minutes
Cooking time: about 35 minutes
Oven temperature: 180°C (350°F), Gas Mark 4

Chocolate Bread and Butter Pudding

An irresistible pudding, combining layers of sweet brioche with melting pockets of dark chocolate sauce. Cinnamon bread or fruited teabread can be used instead of the brioche.

- 200 g/7 oz plain chocolate, broken into pieces
- 50 g/2 oz unsalted butter
- ½ teaspoon ground mixed spice
- 250 g/8 oz brioche
- 3 eggs
- 25 g/1 oz caster sugar
- 600 ml/1 pint milk
- cocoa powder or icing sugar, for dusting

1 Grease a shallow 1.8 litre/3 pint ovenproof dish. Put the chocolate in a heatproof bowl with 25 g/1 oz of the butter and the mixed spice. Place over a pan of simmering water and leave until melted. Stir the ingredients lightly together.

2 Cut the brioche into thin slices. Arrange about a third of the slices in the prepared dish.

3 Place spoonfuls of the chocolate sauce over the bread. Cover with another third of the bread and then the remaining sauce. Arrange the rest of the bread on top.

4 Melt the remaining butter and beat together with the eggs, sugar and milk. Pour over the bread and leave to stand for 30 minutes.

5 Bake in a preheated oven, 180°C (350°F), Gas Mark 4, for about 50 minutes until the crust is golden. Serve the pudding liberally dusted with either cocoa powder or with icing sugar.

Serves 6
Preparation time: 15 minutes, plus standing time
Cooking time: about 50 minutes
Oven temperature: 180°C (350°F), Gas Mark 4

Chocolate Crumble Pudding

Chocolate and ginger have always been happy partners, and this dessert is no exception.

- 375 g/12 oz plain flour
- 1 teaspoon baking powder
- 250 g/8 oz unsalted butter
- 175 g/6 oz caster sugar
- 1 egg
- 2 teaspoons vanilla essence
- 1 teaspoon ground mixed spice
- 200 g/7 oz milk chocolate, roughly chopped
- 125 g/4 oz plain chocolate, roughly chopped
- 2 pieces stem ginger (about 25 g/1 oz)
- 2 tablespoons demerara sugar
- cocoa powder or icing sugar, for dusting
- lightly whipped or clotted cream, to serve

1 Lightly grease a 23 cm/9 inch spring-release cake tin or loose-based cake tin. Sift the flour and baking powder into a bowl.

2 Add the butter, cut into small pieces and rub in with the fingertips until the mixture resembles coarse breadcrumbs. Stir in the caster sugar. Measure 250 g/8 oz of the crumble mixture and reserve.

3 Add the egg, vanilla essence and mixed spice to the remaining mixture, and mix to a firm paste. Press into the base of the prepared tin.

4 Scatter the milk and plain chocolate over the base. Mix the stem ginger with the reserved crumble and spoon it over the chocolate. Sprinkle with the demerara sugar.

5 Bake in a preheated oven, 180°C (350°F), Gas Mark 4, for about 1 hour until the crumble is pale golden. Leave in the tin for 10 minutes; remove and dust with cocoa powder or icing sugar. Serve with whipped or clotted cream.

Serves 8
Preparation time: 20 minutes
Cooking time: about 1 hour
Oven temperature: 180°C (350°F), Gas Mark 4

White Chocolate Cherry Tart

The perfect marriage of chocolate and cherries is both traditional and highly successful.

PASTRY:

- 175 g/6 oz plain flour
- ½ teaspoon ground cinnamon
- 125 g/4 oz unsalted butter
- 25 g/1 oz caster sugar
- 2–3 teaspoons cold water

FILLING:

- 2 eggs
- 40 g/1½ oz caster sugar
- 150 g/5 oz white chocolate, finely chopped
- 300 ml/½ pint double cream
- 450 g/1 lb fresh black or red cherries or 2 x 425 g/14 oz cans pitted black or red cherries
- ground cinnamon, for dusting
- extra cherries, to decorate (optional)

1 Make the pastry. Sift the flour and cinnamon into a bowl. Add the butter, cut into small pieces and rub in with the fingertips. Add the sugar and enough water to mix to a firm dough. Wrap and chill for 30 minutes.

2 Roll out the dough on a floured surface and use to line a 23 cm/9 inch x 2.5 cm/1 inch deep loose-based flan tin. Trim off the excess pastry around the rim.

3 Bake blind in a preheated oven, 200°C (400°F), Gas Mark 6, for 10 minutes. (To bake blind, line the case with greaseproof paper and fill with baking beans.) Lift out the greaseproof paper and baking beans and bake for a further 5 minutes. Reduce the oven temperature to 180°C (350°F), Gas Mark 4.

4 Make the filling. Beat together the eggs and sugar. Heat the chocolate and cream in a small heavy-based saucepan until the chocolate has melted. Pour over the egg mixture, stirring constantly.

5 Stone the cherries, if using fresh, or thoroughly drain the canned cherries. Arrange in the flan case. Pour the chocolate mixture over the cherries.

6 Bake in the oven for about 45 minutes until the chocolate cream is set. Dust with cinnamon and serve warm, decorated with extra cherries if liked.

Serves 6–8
Preparation time: 30 minutes, plus chilling
Cooking time: about 1 hour
Oven temperature: 200°C (400°F), Gas Mark 6, then 180°C (350°F), Gas Mark 4

VARIATION

Dark Chocolate Cherry Tart

Replace 5 g/¼ oz of the flour in the pastry with 5 g/¼ oz cocoa powder. In the chocolate custard, use finely chopped plain chocolate instead of white, and use an extra 25 g/1 oz of caster sugar.

Hot Chocolate Pecan Pie

A rich pudding, grand enough for a dinner party, combining the texture and flavour of pecan nuts with chocolate and maple syrup, served in a chocolate pastry case.

PASTRY:

- 175 g/6 oz plain flour
- 25 g/1 oz cocoa powder
- 125 g/4 oz unsalted butter
- 50 g/2 oz caster sugar
- 2 egg yolks
- 1–2 tablespoons cold water

FILLING:

- 175 g/6 oz caster sugar
- 150 ml/¼ pint maple syrup
- 50 g/2 oz unsalted butter
- 1 teaspoon vanilla essence
- 3 tablespoons cocoa powder
- 3 eggs
- 200 g/7 oz pecan halves, very lightly chopped

TO SERVE:

- crème fraîche
- ground cinnamon or icing sugar

1 Make the pastry. Sift the plain flour and cocoa powder into a bowl. Add the butter, cut into small pieces, and rub in gently with the fingertips until the mixture resembles fine breadcrumbs.

2 Add the sugar, egg yolks and enough cold water to make a firm dough. Knead lightly, then wrap and chill for 30 minutes.

3 Roll out the pastry on a lightly floured surface and use to line a 23 cm/9 inch x 2.5 cm/1 inch deep loose-based flan tin. Trim off excess pastry around the rim.

4 Bake blind in a preheated oven, 200°C (400°F), Gas Mark 6, for 10 minutes. (To bake blind, line the tin with greaseproof paper and fill with baking beans or dried beans.) Lift out the paper and beans and bake for a further 5 minutes. Reduce the oven temperature to 160°C (325°F), Gas Mark 3.

5 Make the filling. Put the sugar and syrup in a small saucepan and heat until the sugar dissolves. Remove from the heat and stir in the butter until melted.

6 Leave to cool slightly, then stir in the vanilla essence, cocoa powder and eggs.

7 Scatter the chopped pecan nuts in the pastry case and pour over the syrup mixture. Bake for about 50 minutes until just set. Serve with spoonfuls of crème fraîche, sprinkled with cinnamon or icing sugar.

Serves 10

Preparation time: 25 minutes, plus chilling
Cooking time: about 1 hour 5 minutes
Oven temperature: 200°C (400°F), Gas Mark 6, then 160°C (325°F), Gas Mark 3

Almondy Chocolate Pithiviers

The rich glaze on this delicious pie is made by dusting the surface with icing sugar during baking.

- 75 g/3 oz unsalted butter, softened
- 3 tablespoons brandy
- 75 g/3 oz ground almonds
- 75 g/3 oz caster sugar
- 2 tablespoons cocoa powder
- 1 egg
- 500 g/1 lb puff pastry
- 125 g/4 oz bar plain or bitter chocolate
- beaten egg, to glaze
- icing sugar, for dusting
- single cream, to serve

1 Grease and dampen a baking sheet. Beat the butter in a bowl with the brandy, almonds and sugar until soft. Beat in the cocoa powder and egg.

2 Cut the pastry into two pieces, one slightly larger than the other. Roll out the smaller piece on a lightly floured surface and cut out a 23 cm/9 inch circle, using a plate as a guide. Transfer to the baking sheet.

3 Spoon half the almond paste to within 2.5 cm/1 inch of the edge of the pastry and level the surface. Arrange the chocolate over the paste, breaking it up to fit. Spread the remaining paste over the top.

4 Brush the rim of the pastry with beaten egg. Roll out the remaining pastry to a 24 cm/9½ inch circle and lay it over the pie, sealing the edges firmly together.

5 Flute the edges of the pastry at 2.5 cm/1 inch intervals with the back of a knife. Chill for 30 minutes.

6 Brush with beaten egg to glaze. Using the tip of a sharp knife, mark faint lines from the centre of the pie to the edges. Bake in a preheated oven, 220°C (425°F), Gas Mark 7, for 30 minutes until risen and golden.

7 Remove from the oven and raise the temperature to 230°C (450°F), Gas Mark 8. Generously dust the pithiviers with the icing sugar and return to the oven for a further 5 minutes until highly glazed. Serve the pie warm with single cream.

Serves 6–8
Preparation time: 25 minutes, plus chilling
Cooking time: 35 minutes
Oven temperature: 220°C (425°F), Gas Mark 7, then 230°C (450°F), Gas Mark 8

VARIATION

Walnut and Chocolate Pithiviers

Finely grind 75 g/3 oz broken walnuts in a food processor or blender until the texture of ground almonds. Beat with the butter, brandy and sugar, then continue as above.

White Chocolate Soufflés

These simple hot soufflés can be served with the Glossy Chocolate Sauce (see page 8) or, for a lighter alternative, the Hot Raspberry Sauce variation right.

- 5 g/¼ oz unsalted butter, melted
- 250 g/8 oz white chocolate, broken into pieces
- 50 ml/2 fl oz double cream
- 25 ml/1 fl oz milk
- 40 g/1½ oz caster sugar
- 6 eggs, separated
- 1 teaspoon vanilla essence
- cocoa powder or icing sugar, for dusting

1 Use the melted unsalted butter to brush and grease the sides of 6 individual 150 ml/¼ pint ovenproof soufflé dishes. Place the dishes on a baking sheet.

2 Put the white chocolate in a heatproof bowl together with the double cream and the milk, and then heat over a pan of simmering water until the chocolate has melted completely. Stir the mixture lightly to blend together.

3 Stir the sugar, egg yolks and vanilla essence into the chocolate and cream mixture. Whisk the egg whites in a large bowl until stiff and with soft but formed peaks. Using a large metal spoon, fold a quarter of the egg whites into the chocolate sauce, then fold in the remainder.

4 Spoon the mixture into the dishes, filling them almost to the rims, and bake in a preheated oven, 200°C (400°F), Gas Mark 6, for 15–20 minutes until well risen and golden. Dust with cocoa powder or icing sugar and serve immediately with the sauce.

Serves 6
Preparation time: 20 minutes
Cooking time: 20 minutes
Oven temperature: 200°C (400°F), Gas Mark 6

VARIATION

Hot Raspberry Sauce

Lightly blend 375 g/12 oz raspberries in a food processor, or mash them thoroughly. Press through a sieve into a bowl. Pour into a saucepan and add 1 tablespoon lemon juice and 2 tablespoons icing sugar. Heat through gently, adding a little more sugar to the sauce, if liked.

Pear Compôte with Chocolate Sabayon

Pears and chocolate go together very well in this fruity compôte with chocolate sauce.

- 12 small or 6 large ripe pears
- 2 tablespoons lemon juice
- 150 g/5 oz caster sugar
- 600 ml/1 pint cold water
- 2 strips pared lemon rind
- 1 cinnamon stick, halved
- 6 cloves
- 4 tablespoons kirsch

SAUCE:

- 50 g/2 oz plain chocolate, broken into pieces
- 3 egg yolks
- 1 tablespoon cocoa powder

1 Peel the pears, leaving the stalks attached and keep whole. Brush with the lemon juice.

2 Put the sugar in a large saucepan with the water. Heat gently, stirring, until the sugar is completely dissolved. Bring to the boil and boil for 2 minutes. Add the pears, lemon rind, cinnamon stick pieces and cloves and cover with a lid. Simmer gently for about 20 minutes, turning once, until the pears are soft.

3 Drain the pears and put in a serving dish. Measure 125 ml/4 fl oz of the syrup. Add the kirsch to the remaining syrup and pour over the pears.

4 Make the sauce. Put the broken plain chocolate in a heatproof bowl over a pan of simmering water and leave until melted.

5 Put the egg yolks in a large heatproof bowl with the cocoa powder. Whisk until well mixed, then place the bowl over a pan of simmering water and continue whisking, gradually adding the measured syrup until foamy.

6 Add the melted chocolate and whisk lightly to combine. Serve warm with the pears.

Serves 6

Preparation time: 25 minutes
Cooking time: about 30 minutes

VARIATIONS

Red Plum Compôte

Halve and stone 750 g/1½ lb plums. Make the syrup as above, omitting the lemon and using 2 strips of pared orange rind. Simmer the plums for 5–10 minutes until softened.

Apricot Compôte

Make the syrup as above, adding an extra 50 g/2 oz caster sugar. Add 750 g/1½ lb whole apricots and simmer for about 10 minutes until the apricots are softened.

Baked Bananas with Chocolate Fudge Sauce

- 4 firm bananas, skins left on
- 1 tablespoon lemon juice

SAUCE:

- 100 ml/3½ fl oz double cream
- 125 g/4 oz plain chocolate, broken into pieces
- 25 g/1 oz unsalted butter
- 125 g/4 oz golden syrup
- lightly whipped cream or vanilla ice cream, to serve

1 Place the bananas in a shallow ovenproof dish. Brush the skins with the lemon juice and bake in a preheated oven, 180°C (350°F), Gas Mark 4, for 20 minutes or until the bananas have darkened in colour and feel softened.

2 Meanwhile, make the sauce. Put the cream, chocolate, butter and golden syrup in a small, heavy-based saucepan. Heat gently, stirring frequently, until the chocolate has melted. Bring to the boil and boil for 2 minutes until thickened slightly.

3 Transfer the bananas to warmed serving plates. Split lengthways to reveal the flesh. Top with cream or ice cream and serve with the hot sauce.

Serves 4

Preparation time: 10 minutes
Cooking time: 20 minutes
Oven temperature: 180°C (350°F), Gas Mark 4

Hot Chocolate Crêpes with Spiced Ricotta and Raisins

CREPES:

- 100 g/3½ oz plain flour
- 15 g/½ oz cocoa powder
- 2 tablespoons caster sugar
- 1 egg
- 300 ml/½ pint milk
- oil, for frying

FILLING:

- 1 piece (about 15 g/½ oz) stem ginger
- 2 tablespoons caster sugar
- 250 g/8 oz ricotta cheese
- 50 g/2 oz raisins
- 150 g/5 oz white chocolate, finely chopped
- 3 tablespoons double cream
- caster sugar, for dusting

TO SERVE:

- Glossy Chocolate Sauce (see page 8)
- single cream

1 Make the crêpes. Sift the flour and cocoa powder into a bowl. Stir in the sugar. Add the egg and a little milk, and whisk to make a stiff batter. Beat in the remaining milk.

2 Heat a little oil in a medium frying pan. Drain off the oil. When the pan is very hot, pour in a little batter and tilt the pan so the batter coats the base. Cook over a moderate heat until browned on the underside.

3 Flip over the crêpe with a palette knife and cook the other side. Slide the crêpe out of the pan and keep warm. Add a little more oil to the pan and make 7 more crêpes.

4 Make the filling. Finely chop the ginger and mix in a bowl with the sugar, ricotta, raisins, chocolate and cream. Place spoonfuls of the filling in the centres of the crêpes. Fold into quarters, enclosing the filling.

5 Place the crêpes in a large shallow ovenproof dish and dust with sugar. Bake in a preheated oven, 200°C (400°F), Gas Mark 6, for 10 minutes until heated through. Serve hot with the Glossy Chocolate Sauce and single cream.

Serves 4

Preparation time: 30 minutes
Cooking time: about 25 minutes
Oven temperature: 200°C (400°F), Gas Mark 6.

VARIATION

Chocolate Crêpes with Almonds and Peaches

Finely chop 125 g/4 oz almond paste and mix with 75 g/3 oz chopped plain chocolate. Halve and stone 4 small ripe peaches. Make the crêpes and fill each with a peach half and a little almond paste and chocolate. Heat as above and serve with single cream.

Marbled Chocolate Pudding with Hazelnut Butter Sauce

The hazelnut sauce on this delicious pudding is the perfect finishing touch.

PUDDING:

- 125 g/4 oz plain chocolate, broken into pieces
- 125 g/4 oz white chocolate, broken into pieces
- 175 g/6 oz unsalted butter, softened
- 175 g/6 oz caster sugar
- 3 eggs, beaten
- 175 g/6 oz self-raising flour, sifted

SAUCE:

- 60 g/2½ oz hazelnuts, toasted
- 75 g/3 oz caster sugar
- 75 ml/3 fl oz water
- 2 tablespoons lemon juice
- 40 g/1½ oz unsalted butter

1 Grease and line the base of a 1.2 litre/2 pint pudding basin. Melt the plain and white chocolate in separate bowls over simmering water.
2 Beat together the butter and sugar until light and creamy. Gradually beat in the eggs, adding a little flour to prevent the mixture curdling.
3 Fold in the remaining flour, then turn half the mixture into a separate bowl. Stir the plain chocolate into one mixture and the white into the other.
4 Place alternate spoonfuls of the white and dark chocolate mixtures into the pudding basin. Level the surface, then swirl a skewer through the mixtures to marble them together.
5 Cover the basin with a double thickness of greaseproof paper, securing under the rim with string. Cover with foil, crumpling this under the rim to seal.
6 Cook the pudding in a steamer for 2–2½ hours, topping up with boiling water if necessary. (Alternatively, position the basin on an upturned saucer in a large saucepan. Pour water into the pan to a depth of about 5 cm/ 2 inches, and cover tightly.)
7 Meanwhile, make the sauce. Roughly chop the hazelnuts. Heat the sugar and water in a small, heavy-based saucepan, stirring until the sugar dissolves. Bring to the boil and boil rapidly until caramel-coloured.
8 Immerse the base of the pan in cold water to prevent further cooking. Add the lemon juice, hazelnuts and butter and heat, stirring until smooth.
9 Invert the pudding on to a serving plate and pour over a little sauce. Serve the remaining sauce separately.

Serves 8
Preparation time: 25 minutes
Cooking time: 2–2½ hours

Fruit and Nut Cinnamon Filos

Leave these pastries to cool slightly before eating. They are equally delicious when served cold, the set chocolate contrasts with the filos.

- 200 g/7 oz fruit and nut chocolate bar
- 8 sheets filo pastry
- 1 egg, beaten
- 40 g/1½ oz caster sugar
- 1 teaspoon ground cinnamon
- oil, for deep frying
- roughly chopped toasted hazelnuts or almonds, to decorate

1 Using a warm knife, cut the chocolate bar widthways into 16 sticks. Lay one sheet of pastry on the work surface and brush with a little beaten egg. Cover with another sheet and brush with more egg. Cut the sheets into 4 rectangles.
2 Place a stick of chocolate on one rectangle of pastry. Fold the two short ends over the ends of the chocolate and brush with more egg.
3 Roll up the pastry so the chocolate is enclosed. Shape the remainder in the same way. Chill for 30 minutes.
4 Mix together the caster sugar and cinnamon. Heat a 5 cm/2 inch depth of oil in a large saucepan to 180–190°C (350–375°F), or until a cube of bread browns in 30 seconds.
5 Add half the pastries and fry for about 2 minutes until golden. Drain on kitchen paper and cook the remainder in the same way. Toss the pastries in the cinnamon sugar and serve scattered with the toasted nuts.

Serves 4
Preparation time: 10 minutes, plus chilling
Cooking time: about 4 minutes

Chocolate Peach Puffs

These quick and easy little pies can be made using white chocolate or, for those with a less sweet tooth, luxury, plain dark chocolate.

- 75 g/3 oz white or plain chocolate, broken into pieces
- 4 small ripe peaches or nectarines
- 375 g/12 oz puff pastry
- beaten egg, to glaze
- icing sugar, for dusting
- chocolate curls, to decorate (see page 7) (optional)
- single cream, to serve

1 Grease and lightly dampen a baking sheet. Put the chocolate in a heatproof bowl over a pan of simmering water and leave until melted.
2 Halve and stone the peaches, then very thinly slice them. Thinly roll out the pastry on a lightly floured surface and cut out 4 x 12 cm/5 inch rounds using a small bowl or saucer as a guide.
3 Place the pastry rounds on the baking sheet. Spoon the melted chocolate on to the pastry, spreading to within 2.5 cm/1 inch of the edges.
4 Arrange the peach slices in an overlapping circle over the chocolate. Make small flutes around the edges of the pastry with the back of a knife.
5 Brush the pastry with a little beaten egg. Bake in a preheated oven, 200°C (400°F), Gas Mark 6, for 15 minutes until the pastry is golden.
6 Dust the pastry and fruit with icing sugar and place under a preheated hot grill for 1–2 minutes, watching closely, until lightly caramelized.
7 Leave to cool slightly, then decorate with chocolate curls, if liked. Serve with single cream.

Serves 4
Preparation time: 20 minutes
Cooking time: 17 minutes
Oven temperature: 200°C (400°F), Gas Mark 6

Chocolate Pancake Stack with Rum Butter

There are many simple variations you can try on this quick and easy pudding. White or plain chocolate, grated orange or walnuts are equally good in the pancakes, while brandy or an orange-flavoured liqueur can be used in the butter.

RUM BUTTER:
- 75 g/3 oz unsalted butter, softened
- 50 g/2 oz icing sugar
- 3 tablespoons rum

PANCAKES:
- 100 g/3½ oz self-raising flour
- 15 g/½ oz cocoa powder
- ½ teaspoon baking powder
- 25 g/1 oz caster sugar
- 1 egg
- 175 ml/6 fl oz milk
- 125 g/4 oz milk chocolate, roughly chopped
- 25 g/1 oz sultanas
- 25 g/1 oz slivered or flaked almonds
- oil, for shallow frying

1 Make the rum butter. Beat the butter in a bowl until soft. Add the icing sugar and the rum and beat together until light and creamy. Transfer to a serving dish.
2 Make the pancakes. Sift the flour, cocoa powder and baking powder into a bowl. Add the sugar. Make a well in the centre, then add the egg and a little of the milk.

3 Whisk the mixture to make a stiff batter, then beat in the remaining milk. Stir in the chocolate, sultanas and almonds.
4 Heat a little oil in a large frying pan or griddle. Take spoonfuls of the batter, making sure you scoop up some fruit, nuts and chocolate each time, and spoon into the pan.
5 Fry gently until just firm and browned on the underside. Turn the pancakes and cook for a further 1 minute. Drain and keep warm while cooking the remainder.
6 Stack the pancakes and top with spoonfuls of the rum butter.

Serves 4–6
Preparation time: 15 minutes
Cooking time: 12–15 minutes

Cold Desserts

Iced Chocolate Mousse

This is like a deliciously rich ice cream, but with an aerated mousse-like texture. You can set it in pretty, freezer-proof serving dishes or in a polythene tub so that it can be scooped on to individual serving plates.

300 g/10 oz plain chocolate, broken into pieces
75 g/3 oz cocoa powder
4 tablespoons golden syrup
4 tablespoons milk
6 eggs
300 ml/½ pint double cream
piped chocolate shapes or small chocolate curls, to decorate (see page 7–8)

1 Put the chocolate pieces in a heatproof bowl with the cocoa powder, syrup and milk. Place over a pan of simmering water and leave until melted. Stir the ingredients lightly together.
2 Place the eggs in a large bowl and whisk until thick and pale. Whip the cream in a separate bowl until just peaking.
3 Add the chocolate mixture to the eggs and fold in, using a large metal spoon.
4 Fold in the cream and turn the mixture into the serving dishes or freezer container. Freeze overnight until firm.
5 If frozen in a large container, scoop out the mousse using an ice cream scoop and re-freeze on a tray until required. Serve decorated with piped chocolate shapes or curls.

Serves 8–10
Preparation time: 20 minutes, plus freezing

1 Beat the mascarpone cheese in a bowl with the brandy, espresso coffee and icing sugar. Reserve 1 tablespoon of the grated chocolate and stir the remainder, together with the single cream, into the mixture.

2 Whip the double cream until just peaking and fold into the mascarpone mixture, using a large metal spoon.

3 Turn the mixture into a freezer container and freeze for 2–3 hours. Using a spoon, scoop the semi-freddo into serving glasses or coffee cups. Drizzle with a little coffee-flavoured liqueur, if liked.

4 Decorate with lightly whipped cream and serve sprinkled with the reserved grated chocolate.

Serves 5–6
Preparation time: 10 minutes, plus freezing

Chocolate Semi-freddo

'Semi-freddo' is a creamy Italian dessert that's quickly assembled and partially frozen. For convenience, you can make it in advance, freeze it and transfer to the refrigerator an hour before serving.

- 250 g/8 oz mascarpone cheese
- 2 tablespoons brandy
- 2 tablespoons fine ground espresso coffee
- 25 g/1 oz icing sugar
- 75 g/3 oz bitter or plain chocolate, grated
- 5 tablespoons single cream
- 300 ml/½ pint double cream

TO DECORATE:

- coffee liqueur (optional)
- lightly whipped cream

Chocolate Flowerpot Creams

A simple name for a sophisticated confection of chocolate, apricots, strawberries, ricotta and Cointreau.

- 125 g/4 oz no-soak dried apricots
- 4 tablespoons Cointreau or other orange-flavoured liqueur
- 250 g/8 oz ricotta cheese
- 300 ml/½ pint double cream
- 2 tablespoons icing sugar
- 125 g/4 oz plain chocolate, finely chopped

TO DECORATE:
- fresh strawberries and apricots
- sprigs of mint or lemon balm
- icing sugar, for dusting

1 Finely chop the apricots and put in a bowl with the orange liqueur. Leave to stand for 2 hours.

2 Line 6 small clean flowerpots, each about 5.5 cm/2¼ inches deep, with squares of dampened muslin.

3 Mix the ricotta in a bowl with the cream, icing sugar and chocolate. Stir in the apricots and liqueur.

4 Pack the mixture into the flowerpots and tap them to level the surfaces. Chill for 2–3 hours.

5 To serve, invert the pots on to serving plates and peel away the muslin. Scatter the fresh fruits around them. Decorate with sprigs of mint or lemon balm and dust with icing sugar.

Serves 6
Preparation time: 20 minutes, plus standing and chilling

Chocolate and Raspberry Bombes

These pretty iced desserts take a little time to prepare, but can be made, decorated and stored in the freezer several days in advance.

ICE CREAM:
- 3 egg yolks
- 1 teaspoon vanilla essence
- 1½ teaspoons cornflour
- 50 g/2 oz caster sugar
- 175 g/6 oz plain chocolate, broken into pieces
- 300 ml/½ pint milk
- 300 ml/½ pint extra thick double cream

TO FINISH:
- 500 g/1 lb good quality raspberry sorbet
- 50 g/2 oz plain chocolate, broken into pieces
- 5 g/¼ oz unsalted butter

TO DECORATE:
- fresh raspberries
- sprigs of mint
- icing sugar, for dusting

1 Make the ice cream. Whisk the egg yolks, vanilla essence, cornflour and sugar in a bowl.
2 Put the chocolate in a saucepan with the milk and heat, stirring until the chocolate has melted. Pour over the egg mixture, whisking well.
3 Pour the mixture back into the saucepan and cook over a gentle heat, stirring, until slightly thickened. Pour into a bowl and cover the surface with greaseproof paper to prevent a skin forming. Leave to cool completely.

4 Whisk the cream into the cooled custard, then turn it into a freezer container. Freeze for several hours or overnight until firm.
5 Remove the ice cream from the freezer and leave to soften for about 30 minutes. Put 6 x 150 ml/¼ pint individual pudding moulds in the freezer for a few minutes until they are very cold.
6 Spread the softened ice cream around the base and sides of the moulds, leaving a cavity in the centre. Re-freeze until firm.
7 Leave the raspberry sorbet to soften at room temperature for about 30 minutes, then pack it into the centre of each mould until level with the ice cream. Re-freeze until firm.

8 Dip each mould very briefly in hot water and twist until loosened. Tap out on to a freezer-proof tray.
9 Put the chocolate in a small bowl with the butter and melt over a pan of simmering water. Place in a small piping bag fitted with a fine writer nozzle and scribble lines or loops of chocolate on to the ice creams. (Alternatively, you can use a paper piping bag and snip off the tip.)
10 Freeze until required, then transfer to serving plates and decorate with raspberries, sprigs of mint and a light dusting of icing sugar.

Serves 6
Preparation time: 1 hour, plus freezing
Cooking time: 2 minutes

Chocolate Velvet Pie

This chocolate shortbread base is an interesting variation on traditional plain shortbread.

SHORTBREAD:

- 175 g/6 oz plain flour
- 2 teaspoons cocoa powder
- 125 g/4 oz unsalted butter
- 25 g/1 oz caster sugar

FILLING:

- 4 teaspoons powdered gelatine
- 3 tablespoons cold water
- 125 g/4 oz caster sugar
- 3 egg yolks
- 1 tablespoon cornflour
- 600 ml/1 pint milk
- 2 tablespoons finely ground espresso coffee
- 350 g/12 oz plain chocolate, broken into pieces

TO DECORATE:

- 300 ml/½ pint double cream
- chocolate caraque (see page 7)

1 Make the shortbread case. Grease a loose base fluted flan tin, measuring 20 cm/8 inches across the base and 5 cm/2 inches deep. Sift the flour and cocoa powder into a bowl. Add the butter, cut into small pieces, and rub in with the fingertips. Add the sugar and mix to a dough.

2 Using your hands, press the shortbread mixture into the base and up the sides of the tin in an even layer. Bake in a preheated oven, 180°C (350°F) Gas Mark 4, for 20 minutes.

Leave the base to cool.

3 Make the filling. Sprinkle the gelatine over the water in a small bowl and leave to soak.

4 Whisk the sugar with the eggs yolks, cornflour and a little of the milk in a bowl. Bring the remaining milk to the boil with the coffee powder then pour it over the egg mixture, whisking well.

5 Return the mixture to the saucepan and heat gently, stirring until thickened. Remove from the heat and beat in the gelatine until dissolved.

6 Add the chocolate and stir until it has melted. Leave to cool slightly then pour the mixture into the flan case. Chill for several hours in the refrigerator until firm.

7 Transfer the pie to a serving plate. Whip the cream until it is stiff enough to hold its shape. Swirl over the top of the pie and scatter generously with chocolate caraque.

Serves 10

Preparation time: 35 minutes, plus chilling
Cooking time: 22 minutes
Oven temperature: 180°C (350°F), Gas Mark 4

Chocoholic's Alaska

Irresistible chocolate sponge, ice cream and sauce are assembled under a casing of meringue in this updated classic. Make this several days in advance and store in the freezer ready for last minute baking.

SPONGE:
- 50 g/2 oz unsalted butter, softened
- 50 g/2 oz caster sugar
- 1 egg
- 40 g/1½ oz self-raising flour, sifted
- ¼ teaspoon baking powder
- 15 g/½ oz cocoa powder
- 2 tablespoons coffee liqueur

TO FINISH:
- 1 litre/1¾ pint round tub chocolate ice cream
- 250 g/8 oz plain chocolate, broken into pieces
- 75 g/3 oz unsalted butter
- 4 egg whites
- 250 g/8 oz caster sugar
- chocolate curls, to decorate (see page 7) (optional)

1 Make the sponge. Grease and line the base of an 18 cm/7 inch round cake tin. Beat together the butter, sugar, egg, flour, baking powder and cocoa powder.
2 Turn into the tin and level the surface. Bake in a preheated oven, 180°C (350°F), Gas Mark 4, for 20–25 minutes until just firm. Transfer to a wire rack to cool.
3 Split the sponge in half horizontally and drizzle with the coffee liqueur. Turn the ice cream out of the tub, keeping it in shape.
4 Using a large knife, slice the block of ice cream in half horizontally.
5 Put one sponge layer on a flat ovenproof serving plate. (Alternatively, use the base of a 20 cm/8 inch round loose base cake or flan tin so that you can lift it on to a decorative plate to serve.)
6 Cover with one half of the ice cream. Cover this with the other half of the sponge then the remaining ice cream. Trim off any excess sponge. Return to the freezer.
7 Put the chocolate in a heatproof bowl with the butter and melt over a pan of simmering water. Stir lightly until smooth. Quickly spread the chocolate in a thin layer all over the ice cream and sponge. Return to the freezer.
8 Whisk the egg whites until stiff. Gradually whisk in the sugar, a little at a time, until stiff and glossy. Spread the meringue over the chocolate sauce to cover. Make soft peaks over the meringue with the back of a spoon. Return to the freezer.
9 Transfer the Alaska to the fridge about 30 minutes before serving. Bake in a preheated oven, 230°C (450°F), Gas Mark 8, for 3–5 minutes, until the meringue is turning golden. Serve immediately, scattered with chocolate curls, if liked.

Serves 10
Preparation time: 40 minutes, plus freezing
Cooking time: about 30 minutes
Oven temperature: 180°C (350°F), Gas Mark 4, then 230°C (450°F), Gas Mark 8

White Chocolate Creams with Orange and Cranberry Sauce

Cranberries give these creams an interesting bite.

- 2 teaspoons powdered gelatine
- 2 tablespoons cold water
- 4 egg yolks
- 25 g/1 oz caster sugar
- 1 teaspoon cornflour
- 1 teaspoon vanilla essence
- 300 ml/½ pint milk
- 200 g/7 oz white chocolate, chopped
- 300 ml/½ pint double cream

SAUCE:

- 3 clementines or 2 small oranges
- 125 g/4 oz fresh or frozen cranberries
- 75 g/3 oz caster sugar
- 150 ml/¼ pint cold water
- chocolate leaves or piped chocolate decorations (see page 7-8), to decorate

1 Lightly oil 6 individual 150 ml/¼ pint ramekin dishes, pudding basins or metal moulds.

2 Sprinkle the gelatine over the water in a small bowl. Whisk the egg yolks in a bowl with the sugar, cornflour, vanilla essence and a little of the milk.

3 Bring the remaining milk to the boil in a heavy-based saucepan. Pour over the egg mixture, stirring.

4 Return to the saucepan and heat gently, stirring until the mixture is slightly thickened. (Do not allow to boil or the mixture might curdle.)

5 Remove from the heat and stir in the gelatine until dissolved. Add the chocolate and stir until melted. Leave to cool.

6 Whip the cream until just peaking. Using a large metal spoon fold the cream into the custard. Spoon the mixture into the prepared containers. Place on a tray and chill for 4–5 hours or overnight.

7 Make the sauce. Pare thin strips of rind from one of the clementines and cut into fine shreds. Remove the peel from all the fruit and thinly slice.

8 Put the cranberries in a small, heavy-based saucepan with the sugar and water. Heat gently until the sugar dissolves and then simmer until the cranberries have softened. Drain the cranberries.

9 Boil the liquid until very syrupy, then return the cranberries to the pan with the sliced clementines and shredded rind. Mix together and turn into a small bowl. Leave to cool.

10 Dip the chocolate moulds very briefly into cold water to loosen, then invert on to serving plates. Spoon a little sauce over and around the creams and serve decorated with chocolate leaves or piped decorations.

Serves 6
Preparation time: 30 minutes, plus cooling
Cooking time: about 10 minutes

Amaretti and Chocolate Trifle

CUSTARD:

- 2 egg yolks
- 2 tablespoons cocoa powder
- 1 teaspoon cornflour
- 50 g/2 oz caster sugar
- 150 ml/¼ pint milk
- 300 ml/½ pint double cream
- 200 g/7 oz plain chocolate, broken
  into pieces

TO FINISH:

- 50 g/2 oz caster sugar
- 50 ml/2 fl oz cold water
- 1 teaspoon vanilla essence
- 750 g/1½ lb fresh apricots, halved
  and stoned
- 175 g/6 oz amaretti biscuits
- 4 tablespoons Amaretto di Saronno liqueur
- 50 g/2 oz blanched almonds, toasted
- 300 ml/½ pint double cream
- cocoa powder, for dusting

TO DECORATE:

- chocolate leaves (see page 7)
- sugared almonds, coarsely chopped

1 Make the custard. Lightly whisk the egg yolks with the cocoa powder, cornflour, sugar and half the milk.
2 Put the remaining milk in a saucepan with the cream and chocolate. Heat gently, stirring, until the chocolate has melted. Bring almost to the boil, then pour it over the egg mixture, whisking well.
3 Return the custard to the saucepan and whisk well over a moderate heat until the custard has thickened slightly. Transfer to a bowl and cover

the surface with greaseproof paper to prevent a skin forming. Leave to cool.
4 Heat the sugar and water in a saucepan until the sugar dissolves. Add the vanilla and apricots, and cover with a lid. Simmer gently for 2–5 minutes (depending on the ripeness of the fruit) until just softened.
5 Drain the apricots, reserving 3 tablespoons of the syrup. Place the apricots in a glass serving dish. Scatter the biscuits over the apricots.
6 Mix the reserved syrup with the

liqueur and spoon over the biscuits. Scatter with the almonds. Spoon the cooled custard into the dish and leave to stand for several hours to set.
7 Whip the cream until just peaking. Spoon over the custard and dust with cocoa powder. Decorate the trifle with chocolate leaves and sugared almonds.

Serves 8–10
Preparation time: 30 minutes,
plus standing time
Cooking time: about 7 minutes

Chocolate and Hazelnut Meringue Pie

This impressive dessert is actually surprisingly easy to make.

PASTRY:

- 175 g/6 oz plain flour
- 75 g/3 oz unsalted butter
- 25 g/1 oz plain chocolate, grated
- 25 g/1 oz icing sugar
- 1 egg
- 1–2 teaspoons cold water

FILLING:

- 50 g/2 oz cornflour
- 3 egg yolks
- 25 g/1 oz caster sugar
- 1 teaspoon vanilla essence
- 600 ml/1 pint milk
- 175 g/6 oz plain chocolate, chopped

MERINGUE:

- 3 egg whites
- 175 g/6 oz caster sugar
- 25 g/1 oz hazelnuts, toasted and finely chopped
- pouring cream, to serve

1 Make the pastry. Sift the flour into a bowl. Add the butter, cut into small pieces and rub in with the fingertips.
2 Stir in the chocolate, icing sugar, egg yolk and enough water to mix to a firm dough. Knead lightly, then wrap and chill for 30 minutes.
3 Roll out the pastry on a lightly floured surface and use to line a 23 cm/9 inch plain or fluted flan ring set on a baking sheet.

4 Bake blind in a preheated oven, 200°C (400°F),Gas Mark 6, for 15 minutes. (To bake blind, line the tin with greaseproof paper and fill with baking beans or dried beans.) Lift out the paper and beans and bake for a further 5 minutes.
5 Make the filling. Mix together the cornflour, egg yolks, sugar, vanilla essence and a little of the milk in a large bowl. Bring the remaining milk to the boil in a saucepan. Pour over the egg mixture, stirring.
6 Return the mixture to the saucepan and cook for 2 minutes, stirring until thickened. Add the chopped chocolate and stir until melted. Pour the mixture into the pastry case.
7 Make the meringue. Whisk the egg whites until stiff. Gradually whisk in the sugar, a little at a time, until the mixture is stiff and glossy. Stir the hazelnuts into the meringue
8 Spoon the meringue over the pie, shaping peaks with the back of a spoon. Place under a preheated hot grill for about 2 minutes until the peaks are golden. Serve warm or cold with pouring cream.

Serves 8
Preparation time: 40 minutes, plus chilling
Cooking time: 25 minutes
Oven temperature: 200°C (400°F), Gas Mark 6

VARIATION

Chocolate and Orange Meringue Pie

Use 200 g/7 oz chopped white chocolate in place of the plain in the filling, and omit the caster sugar. Replace the chopped hazelnuts in the meringue with the finely grated rind of 1 small orange.

Spiced Pavlova with Caramel Oranges

This is a rich, extravagant dessert, suitable for even the grandest occasion.

- 5 egg whites
- 300 g/10 oz caster sugar
- ½ teaspoon ground mixed spice
- 2 teaspoons cornflour
- 2 teaspoons white wine vinegar

FILLING:

- 450 ml/¾ pint double cream
- 175 g/6 oz plain chocolate, broken into pieces
- 3 tablespoons Cointreau or other orange-flavoured liqueur
- 2 small oranges, with peel left on
- 600 ml/1 pint cold water
- 250 g/8 oz caster sugar

TO DECORATE:

- double chocolate shavings (see page 7)
- cocoa powder, for dusting

1 Draw a 25 cm/10 inch circle on a piece of greaseproof paper and invert on to a baking sheet.

2 Whisk the egg whites in a bowl until stiff. Gradually whisk in the sugar, a little at a time until the mixture is stiff and glossy. Whisk in the spice then fold in the cornflour and vinegar.

3 Turn the mixture into the marked circle and spread to the edges, forming large peaks with the back of a spoon.

4 Bake in a preheated oven, 150°C (300°F), Gas Mark 2, for 5 minutes. Reduce the oven temperature to 120°C (250°F), Gas Mark ½ and bake for a further 1–1¼ hours until crisp. Cool on the baking sheet.

5 Make the filling. Put 150 ml/¼ pint of the cream in a small saucepan with the chocolate and cook gently, stirring, until it has melted. Remove from the heat and transfer to a bowl. Stir in the liqueur and leave to cool.

6 Thinly slice the oranges. Put the water and sugar in a heavy-based saucepan and heat gently, stirring, until the sugar dissolves. Bring to the boil for 2 minutes. Add the orange slices and simmer gently for about 25 minutes until the rind is tender.

7 Whip the remaining cream until just holding its shape. Put the meringue on a large flat serving plate.

8 Whisk the chocolate cream until just peaking and spoon around the top of the pavlova. Pile the plain whipped cream into the centre.

9 Pile the drained orange slices and chocolate shavings on the pavlova. Lightly dust with cocoa powder.

Serves 10

Preparation time: 45 minutes
Cooking time: 1½–1¾ hours
Oven temperature: 150°C (300°F), Gas Mark 2, then 120°C (250°F), Gas Mark ½

VARIATION

Spiced Pavlova with Tropical Fruits

Use brandy or rum instead of the orange liqueur. Omit the oranges in syrup. Use 1 peeled, seeded and sliced papaya, 1 peeled, stoned and sliced mango, and the pulp from 2 passionfruit on top of the pavlova. Decorate with chocolate curls and cape gooseberries.

Chocolate 'Vases' with Fruit Salad

Chocolate has a unique 'sculptural' quality, in that it can be melted and set into decorative shapes like these stunning containers for fruits, mousses or cold custards. Make them 2– 3 days ahead and fill them on the day you serve them.

- 175 g/6 oz plain or milk chocolate, broken into pieces
- 1 lemon
- 175 g/6 oz strawberries
- 125 g/4 oz lychees or grapes
- 50 g/2 oz blueberries

- 75 ml/3 fl oz dessert wine
- 150 ml/¼ pint double cream
- 2 tablespoons icing sugar

TO DECORATE:

- sprigs of mint
- icing sugar, for dusting (optional)

1 Put the chocolate in a heatproof bowl over a saucepan of simmering water and leave until melted.

2 Cut out 6 x 20 cm/8 inch squares of heavy-duty foil. Cut one end off the lemon so that it can stand upright. Place the lemon on the centre of one square of foil and bring up the sides of the foil around the lemon, pressing the folds firmly against the lemon to give a smooth case and letting the ends splay out at the top. (Alternatively you can use a metal dariole mould to shape the cases.)

3 Lift out the lemon and make 5 more cases in the same way. Spoon a little chocolate into the base of one case and spread it up the sides to within 1 cm/½ inch of the edges of the foil. Fill the remaining cases in the same way. Chill the cases until set.

4 Meanwhile halve any large strawberries. Peel and stone the lychees and mix the fruits in a bowl. Pour the wine over the fruits and leave to macerate for at least 1 hour.

5 Drain the fruits, reserving the wine. Squeeze 1 tablespoon of juice from the lemon and put in a bowl with the cream and icing sugar.

6 Whip the cream until just peaking, then gradually whisk in the reserved wine.

7 Take one chocolate case out of the fridge at a time and carefully peel away the foil. Spoon the cream into the cases and pile the fruits over the cream. Chill for up to 2 hours and decorate with sprigs of mint. Serve dusted with icing sugar, if liked.

Serves 6

Preparation time: 35 minutes, plus chilling

Chocolate and Coffee Burnt Creams

A sophisticated blend of plain chocolate and espresso coffee made richly smooth with double cream !

- 4 egg yolks
- 50 g/2 oz caster sugar
- 450 ml/¾ pint double cream
- 4 teaspoons finely ground espresso coffee
- 200 g/7 oz plain chocolate, finely chopped
- chocolate-coated coffee beans, to decorate

1 Lightly whisk the egg yolks in a bowl with 15 g/½ oz of the sugar.
2 Put the cream, coffee and chocolate in a saucepan and heat gently until the chocolate has melted.
3 Pour the chocolate mixture over the egg yolks, whisking well. Pour the mixture into 4 individual 150 ml/¼ pint ramekins or ovenproof dishes.
4 Place the dishes on a rack in a roasting tin. Pour boiling water into the tin to come 1 cm/½ inch up the sides of the dishes. Bake in a preheated oven, 200°C (400°F), Gas Mark 6, for 15 minutes, or until a skin has formed over the chocolate. Cool.

5 Sprinkle the remaining sugar over the chocolate creams. Place under a preheated hot grill and cook for about 3 minutes until the sugar caramelizes. Leave to cool. Serve decorated with chocolate-coated coffee beans.

Serves 4
Preparation time: 15 minutes, plus cooling
Cooking time: 18–20 minutes
Oven temperature: 200°C (400°F), Gas Mark 6

VARIATION
Chocolate Banana Creams

Thinly slice 2 bananas and toss in 1 tablespoon of lemon juice and 1 tablespoon of caster sugar. Place in 6 individual 150 ml/¼ pint ramekins or ovenproof dishes. Make the chocolate custard as above, omitting the espresso coffee powder, and pour over the bananas. Cook and finish as in the main recipe.

Iced Chocolate and Fig Terrine

Iced plain chocolate and figs are an unusual combination in this spectacular terrine.

- 2 tablespoons coffee granules
- 175 ml/6 fl oz boiling water
- 175 g/6 oz dried figs
- 600 ml/1 pint double cream
- 5 tablespoons Tia Maria or other coffee-flavoured liqueur
- 300 g/10 oz plain chocolate, broken into pieces
- 50 g/2 oz unsalted butter
- chocolate leaves or twists, to decorate (see pages 7–8)

1 Line the base and sides of a 900 g/ 2 lb loaf tin, preferably with drop sides, with cling film. Mix the coffee with the water and add the figs. Leave for 24 hours.

2 Whip 350 ml/12 fl oz of the cream with 2 tablespoons of the coffee - flavoured liqueur until peaking. Spread into the base and up the sides of the prepared tin to make a case. Freeze for several hours until firm.

3 Drain the figs, reserving the liquid. Put the liquid in a heatproof bowl with the chocolate and butter and melt over a pan of simmering water. Remove from the heat and add the remaining liqueur. Stir together lightly to make a smooth sauce.

4 Whip the remaining double cream until just peaking. Stir in the chocolate sauce and figs and mix carefully until everything is evenly combined.

5 Spoon the mixture into the cream lined tin and level the surface. Freeze for several hours or overnight until firm. Transfer to the refrigerator about 1 hour before serving.

6 Invert the terrine out of the tin and peel away the cling film. Decorate with plenty of chocolate leaves or twists and serve sliced.

Serves 8
Preparation time: 25 minutes, plus soaking and freezing

Gâteaux
and Torte

Fruit and Nut Chocolate Roulade

125 g/4 oz raisins

4 tablespoons Cointreau or other
orange-flavoured liqueur

175 g/6 oz plain chocolate, broken into pieces

5 eggs, separated

150 g/5 oz caster sugar

75 g/3 oz unblanched hazelnuts,
toasted and chopped

TO FINISH:

150 ml/¼ pint double cream

150 ml/¼ pint Greek yogurt

chocolate curls, to decorate

(see pages 7-8)

icing sugar, for dusting

1 Grease and line a 33 x 23 cm/13 x 9 inch Swiss roll tin with greaseproof paper. Grease the paper. Put the raisins and liqueur in a bowl and leave to soak for 2–3 hours.

2 Drain the raisins, reserving the liqueur. Put the chocolate in a bowl and leave over a pan of simmering water until melted. Whisk the egg yolks and sugar together in a bowl until thick and pale. Beat in the melted chocolate, then the raisins and nuts.

3 Whisk the egg whites in a separate bowl until stiff. Using a large metal spoon, fold the egg whites into the yolks mixture.

4 Pour into the prepared tin and spread into the corners. Bake in a preheated oven, 180°C (350°F), Gas Mark 4, for 20–25 minutes until well risen and just firm.

5 Sprinkle a sheet of greaseproof paper with caster sugar. Invert the roulade on to the paper and peel away the lining paper. Cover with a damp tea towel and leave to cool.

6 Whip the cream with the reserved liqueur until peaked. Stir in the yogurt, spread over the roulade and roll up from a short end. Decorate with chocolate curls and icing sugar.

Serves 8

Preparation time: 25 minutes, plus soaking and cooling
Cooking time: 20–25 minutes
Oven temperature: 180°C (350°F), Gas Mark 4

Chocolate Fudge and Coconut Cake

In this unusual recipe, chocolate combines with fudge and coconut, with spectacular results.

- 175 g/6 oz unsalted butter
- 175 g/6 oz caster sugar
- 150 g/5 oz plain flour
- 1 teaspoon baking powder
- 3 eggs
- 125 g/4 oz desiccated coconut
- 2 teaspoons vanilla essence
- 3 tablespoons milk

FILLING:

- 175 g/6 oz plain chocolate, broken into pieces
- 75 g/3 oz unsalted butter
- 150 g/5 oz icing sugar
- 2 tablespoons milk

TO DECORATE:

- 200 g/7 oz plain chocolate, broken into pieces
- 25 g/1 oz unsalted butter
- chocolate curls (see page 7)
- toasted coconut curls
- cocoa powder, for dusting

1 Grease and line the bases of 2 x 20 cm/8 inch round sandwich tins. Cream together the butter and sugar until softened.

2 Sift the flour and baking powder into the bowl. Add the eggs, coconut, vanilla essence and milk. Beat until light and creamy.

3 Turn into the prepared tins and level the surfaces. Bake in a preheated oven, 180°C (350°F), Gas Mark 4, for about 25 minutes until risen and just firm to touch. Transfer to a wire rack to cool.

4 Make the filling. Put the chocolate and butter in a heatproof bowl over a saucepan of simmering water and leave until melted. Remove the bowl from the heat and beat in the icing sugar and milk.

5 Leave the mixture until cool enough to form soft peaks. Split each cake horizontally into 2 layers.

6 Place one layer on a plate and spread with a quarter of the filling. Cover with a second layer of sponge and more filling. Repeat the layering, finishing with a layer of sponge so that you have a quarter of the filling left. Spread this around the sides of the cake to fill in any gaps.

7 To decorate the cake, put the chocolate and butter in a heatproof bowl over a saucepan of simmering water and leave until melted. Stir the melted chocolate lightly and leave to cool until it thickly coats the back of a spoon.

8 Pour the melted chocolate over the top of the cake, easing it around the sides with a palette knife until completely coated.

9 Decorate the top of the cake with chocolate curls and toasted coconut curls and leave to set. Serve dusted with cocoa powder.

Serves 12–14
Preparation time: 45 minutes, plus cooling
Cooking time: about 25 minutes
Oven temperature: 180°C (350°F), Gas Mark 4

Chocolate Truffle Gâteau

Here, layers of plain, milk and white chocolate cream are enclosed in a case of light sponge.

- 2 eggs
- 50 g/2 oz caster sugar
- 50 g/2 oz plain flour

FILLING:

- 450 ml/¾ pint double cream
- 175 g/6 oz milk chocolate, chopped
- 450 ml/¾ pint Greek yogurt
- 175 g/6 oz white chocolate, chopped
- 175 g/6 oz plain chocolate, chopped
- cocoa powder, for dusting
- double quantity Chocolate Modelling Paste (see page 9)

1 Grease and line the base of a 23 cm/9 in loose-bottomed cake tin or spring release tin. Put the eggs and sugar in a heatproof bowl over a saucepan of simmering water. Whisk until the mixture is thick enough to leave a trail when the whisk is lifted from the bowl. Remove from the heat and whisk until cool.

2 Sift the flour into the bowl and fold in using a large metal spoon. Turn into the prepared tin and bake in a preheated oven, 190°C (375°F), Gas Mark 5 for about 15 minutes until risen and just firm to the touch. Transfer to a wire rack and let cool.

3 Clean the tin and line the sides with fresh paper. Cut the sponge in half horizontally. Lay one half in the tin.

4 Make the filling. Bring 150 ml/¼ pint of the cream to the boil in a small saucepan. Remove from the heat and stir in the milk chocolate until melted. Turn into a bowl and stir in 150 ml/ ¼ pint of the yogurt until smooth.

5 Spoon the milk chocolate mixture over the sponge in the tin, spreading until level. Chill until beginning to set.

6 Using another 150 ml/¼ pint of the cream and yogurt, and the white chocolate, make a second chocolate layer and spread over the milk chocolate. Leave until just setting.

7 Use the remaining cream, yogurt and plain chocolate to make a third layer and spread over the white chocolate. Cover with the remaining sponge and chill for 2–3 hours.

8 Remove the gâteau from the tin and transfer to a serving plate, peeling away the paper. Dredge the top of the cake with cocoa powder.

9 Cut the modelling paste into 5 even-sized pieces. Roll 4 pieces very thinly into 12 cm/5 inch rounds, dusting the surface with cocoa powder if the paste sticks. Cut each round in half. Press the curved edge of each semi-circle between thumb and finger to make it wavy. Arrange the 8 shaped pieces right round the gâteau with the straight edges sitting on the plate.

10 Use the remaining modelling paste to shape some roses and ribbons (see page 8). Arrange on top of the cake.

Serves 12

Preparation time: about 1 hour, plus cooling
Cooking time: about 15 minutes
Oven temperature: 190°C (375°F), Gas Mark 5

White Chocolate Gâteau

The sugared rose petals decorating this cake enhance the subtle rosewater flavouring. Lightly brush fresh rose petals with beaten egg white and dust them with caster sugar. Leave to dry on non-stick greaseproof paper for 1 or 2 hours before using.

- 4 eggs
- 125 g/4 oz caster sugar
- 125 g/4 oz plain flour
- 50 g/2 oz white chocolate, finely grated

TO FINISH:

- 3 tablespoons rosewater
- 150 ml/¼ pint crème fraîche
- 200 g/7 oz white chocolate, broken into pieces
- 75 g/3 oz unsalted butter
- 3 tablespoons single cream
- 125 g/4 oz icing sugar
- white chocolate curls or twists (see pages 7–8)
- sugared rose petals (optional)
- icing sugar, for dusting

1 Grease and line the bases of 2 x 20 cm/8 inch round sandwich tins. Put the eggs and sugar in a large heatproof bowl over a pan of simmering water and whisk until the mixture is thick enough to leave a trail when the whisk is lifted from the bowl. Remove from the heat and whisk until cool.
2 Sift the flour into the bowl. Add the grated chocolate and fold in using a large metal spoon.

3 Turn into the prepared tins and bake in a preheated oven, 180°C (350°F), Gas Mark 4, for 20–25 minutes until just firm to the touch. Transfer to a wire rack to cool.
4 Stir the rosewater into the crème fraîche and use to sandwich the 2 cakes together on a serving plate.
5 Put the white chocolate and butter in a heatproof bowl over a saucepan of simmering water and leave until melted. Stir in the cream and icing sugar, and beat until smooth.
6 Leave the mixture to cool until it forms soft peaks, then spread over the top and sides of the cake using a palette knife.
7 Decorate the top of the cake with chocolate curls or twists, sugared rose petals, if using, and a light dusting of icing sugar.

Serves 12
Preparation time: 45 minutes, plus cooling
Cooking time: 20–25 minutes
Oven temperature: 180°C (350°F), Gas Mark 4

Dobos Torte

This is a gloriously ambitious recipe, which is well worth the trouble if you have the time.

- 5 eggs
- 150 g/5 oz caster sugar
- 2 teaspoons vanilla essence
- 150 g/5 oz plain flour

CREME PATISSIERE:

- 1 tablespoon cornflour
- 2 egg yolks
- 75 g/3 oz caster sugar
- 15 g/½ oz cocoa powder
- 300 ml/½ pint milk
- 150 ml/¼ pint double cream
- 250 g/8 oz plain chocolate, broken into pieces

TO DECORATE:

- 125 g/4 oz caster sugar
- 4 tablespoons cold water

1 Mark out 6 x 18 cm/7 inch circles on non-stick greaseproof paper. Invert 3 of the circles on to baking sheets, and grease lightly.

2 Put the eggs and sugar in a heatproof bowl over a saucepan of simmering water and beat until the whisk leaves a trail when lifted from the mixture. Remove the mixture from the heat and whisk until cool.

3 Stir in the vanilla essence. Sift the flour and fold into the mixture. Spoon half the mixture on to the 3 circles, spreading it almost to the edges.

4 Bake in a preheated oven, 200°C (400°F), Gas Mark 6, for 6–8 minutes until just firm. Slide off the baking sheets and line the sheets with the remaining paper. Bake the remaining mixture in the same way.

5 Make the crème pâtissière. Beat the cornflour in a bowl with the egg yolks, sugar, cocoa and a little of the milk. Put the remaining milk in a pan with the cream and bring just to the boil.

6 Whisk into the egg mixture, return to the saucepan and bring to the boil, whisking until thickened. Cover the surface with greaseproof paper to prevent a skin forming. Let cool.

7 Place one layer of the sponge on a serving plate and spread with 3 tablespoons of the custard. Cover with another layer of sponge. Repeat, finishing with a layer of sponge.

8 Put the chocolate in a heatproof bowl and leave over a saucepan of simmering water until melted. Stir into the remaining crème pâtissière.

9 Using a palette knife, spread the mixture over the top and sides of the cake until evenly covered.

10 To make the caramel decorations, lightly oil a large baking sheet. Put the sugar and water in a small heavy-based saucepan and heat gently until the sugar dissolves. Bring to the boil and boil until the syrup has turned a deep caramel colour.

11 Dip the base of the pan in cold water to prevent further cooking. Using a teaspoon, drizzle decorative shapes on to the prepared baking sheet, each about 7.5 cm/3 inches in diameter. Leave the shapes to harden, then arrange on top of the cake.

Serves 14
Preparation time: about 1 hour, plus cooling
Cooking time: 20–25 minutes
Oven temperature: 200°C (400°F), Gas Mark 6

Chocolate Mousse Cake with Frosted Blueberries

Rather like a hot soufflé, this moist cake deflates after baking to produce its characteristic cracked, sugary crust. Decorate with the sugared frosted berries or other seasonal fruits and serve with lightly whipped cream.

- 250 g/8 oz plain chocolate, broken into pieces
- 50 g/2 oz unsalted butter
- 2 tablespoons brandy
- 6 eggs, separated
- 75 g/3 oz caster sugar

TO DECORATE:
- 275 g/9 oz large blueberries
- 1 tablespoon lightly beaten egg white
- 50 g/2 oz caster sugar
- chocolate caraque (see page 7) (optional)

1 Grease and line a 23 cm/9 inch spring-release cake tin. Put the chocolate in a heatproof bowl with the butter and heat over a pan of simmering water until it has melted. Remove from the heat and stir in the brandy.

2 Whisk the egg yolks in a large bowl with 50 g/2 oz of the caster sugar until thickened and pale. Stir in the chocolate mixture.

3 Whisk the egg whites in a separate bowl until stiff. Gradually whisk in the remaining sugar.

4 Using a large metal spoon, fold a quarter of the egg whites into the chocolate mixture, then fold in the remainder.

5 Turn into the prepared tin and bake in a preheated oven, 160°C (325°F), Gas Mark 3, for 35 minutes or until well risen and beginning to crack on the surface. Leave to cool in the tin.

6 Toss the blueberries in a bowl with the egg white until moistened. Turn out on to a tray lined with greaseproof paper and spread to a single layer. Scatter with the sugar and leave to dry.

7 Transfer the cake to a serving plate, peeling away the lining paper. Pile the frosted blueberries on the cake and decorate, if liked, with chocolate caraque.

Serves 8
Preparation time: 25 minutes
Cooking time: about 35 minutes
Oven temperature: 160°C (325°F), Gas Mark 3

VARIATION

Chocolate Mousse Cake with Hot Blueberry Sauce

Make the cake as left and serve with this hot blueberry sauce. Blend 2 teaspoons of cornflour with 3 tablespoons of water in a saucepan. Add another 150 ml/¼ pint water, 75 g/3 oz of caster sugar, the finely grated rind of 1 lemon and 500 g/1 lb of fresh or frozen blueberries. Stir over a gentle heat until slightly thickened.

Chocolate Praline Gâteau

- 250 g/8 oz plain chocolate, broken into pieces
- 75 ml/3 fl oz Amaretto di Saronno liqueur
- 175 g/6 oz unsalted butter, softened
- 175 g/6 oz caster sugar
- 4 eggs
- 125 g/4 oz self-raising flour
- 125 g/4 oz ground almonds

FILLING:

- 250 g/8 oz fresh cherries or 475 g/15 oz canned cherries
- 150 ml/¼ pint double cream

TO DECORATE:

- 3 tablespoons cherry or apricot jam
- 500 g/1 lb white almond paste
- 75 g/3 oz milk or white chocolate, broken

- several fresh cherries or Cape gooseberries
- 175 g/6 fl oz double cream
- 175 g/6 oz plain chocolate, broken

1 Grease and line a 23 cm/9 inch round cake tin. Put the chocolate and liqueur into a heatproof bowl over a saucepan of simmering water and leave until melted. Stir lightly.

2 Cream together the butter and sugar until softened. Add the eggs. Sift the flour into the bowl. Add the almonds and chocolate mixture and stir all the ingredients together until smooth.

3 Turn into the prepared tin and bake in a preheated oven, 160°C (325°F), Gas Mark 3, for 1–1¼ hours until a skewer, inserted into the centre, comes out clean. Leave to cool in the tin.

4 Make the filling. Stone fresh cherries or thoroughly drain canned ones, if using.

5 Whip the cream until it peaks; stir in the cherries. Cut the cake in half horizontally and sandwich with the cherry cream. Place on a serving plate.

6 Prepare the decoration. Melt the jam and press through a sieve. Brush over the top and sides of the cake.

7 Roll out the almond paste on a surface dusted with icing sugar to a 30 cm/12 inch round. Lift over the cake and ease round the sides, trimming off any excess at the base.

8 Put the milk or white chocolate in a heatproof bowl over a pan of simmering water and leave until melted. Half dip the fresh cherries or Cape gooseberries into the chocolate, letting any excess drip back into the bowl. Leave on a lined tray until set. Put the remaining chocolate in a piping bag fitted with a writing nozzle.

9 Bring the cream just to the boil in a saucepan. Remove from the heat and stir in the plain chocolate until melted. Leave to cool slightly, then whisk until beginning to thicken.

10 Spread the plain chocolate mixture over the top and sides of the cake. Using the piping bag, pipe scallops of chocolate round the sides, drawing a cocktail stick through each loop to give a feathered finish. Arrange the dipped fruits on top of the cake.

Serves 16

Preparation time: 1 hour, plus cooling
Cooking time: 1–1¼ hours
Oven temperature: 160°C (325°F), Gas Mark 3

Chocolate Cappuccino Slice

- 3 eggs
- 75 g/3 oz caster sugar
- 75 g/3 oz plain flour
- 1 tablespoon finely ground espresso coffee

CREME PATISSIERE:

- 1 tablespoon cornflour
- 2 egg yolks
- 75 g/3 oz caster sugar
- 1 tablespoon finely ground espresso coffee
- 15 g/½ oz cocoa powder
- 450 ml/¾ pint milk
- 4 tablespoons Kahlua or other coffee-flavoured liqueur

TO DECORATE:

- 175 g/6 oz plain or milk chocolate, broken into pieces
- 300 ml/½ pint double cream
- chocolate curls (see page 7)
- drinking chocolate, for dusting

1 Grease and line a 33 x 23 cm/13 x 9 inch Swiss roll tin. Whisk the eggs and sugar in a large heatproof bowl over a saucepan of simmering water until the mixture is thick enough to leave a trail when the whisk is lifted. Remove from the heat and whisk until cool.

2 Sift the flour and coffee into the bowl and fold in, using a metal spoon. Turn into the tin and ease into the corners. Bake in a preheated oven, 200°C (400°F), Gas Mark 6, for about 12 minutes until just firm to the touch.

3 Sprinkle greaseproof paper with caster sugar and invert the sponge on to it. Peel away the lining paper and leave to cool.

4 Make the crème pâtissière. Mix together the cornflour, egg yolks, sugar, espresso, cocoa and a little of the milk. Bring the remaining milk to the boil and pour over the egg mixture, whisking well.

5 Return to the pan and bring to the boil, whisking until thickened. Transfer to a bowl and cover with greaseproof paper. Leave to cool.

6 Cut the sponge widthways into 3 even-sized rectangles. Place one layer on a serving plate.

7 Beat the Kahlua into the crème patissière. Spread one-third over the sponge. Cover with a second sponge and more custard, then the remaining sponge. Use the remaining custard to cover the cake's top and sides.

8 Prepare the decoration. Put the chocolate in a heatproof bowl over a saucepan of simmering water. Leave until the chocolate has melted.

9 Meanwhile, measure the circumference of the cake and cut a strip of greasepoof paper 1 cm/½ inch longer and 8.5 cm/3½ inches wide.

10 Spread the melted chocolate down the strip, taking the chocolate right to one long edge and giving the other long edge a more wavy decorative finish for the top edge of the cake.

11 Lift the ends of the strip and wrap it around the cake. Chill for about 10 minutes to set. Peel away the paper.

12 Whip the cream until it peaks and pile on to the sponge. Sprinkle chocolate curls over and dust with drinking chocolate.

Serves 10

Preparation time: about 1 hour, plus cooling
Cooking time: about 15 minutes
Oven temperature: 200°C (400°F), Gas Mark 6.

Easy Cakes and Muffins

Fruited Chocolate Cake

250 g/8 oz unsalted butter or margarine, softened

250 g/8 oz light muscovado sugar

275 g/9 oz plain flour

25 g/1 oz cocoa powder

1 teaspoon ground mixed spice

4 eggs

200 g/7 oz mixed nuts, such as Brazil nuts, almonds
and hazelnuts, roughly chopped

250 g/8 oz milk chocolate, chopped

100 g/3½ oz chopped glacé ginger

250 g/8 oz mixed dried fruit

1 Grease and line a 20 cm/8 inch round cake tin. Cream the butter and sugar together in a bowl until softened.

2 Sift the flour, cocoa and mixed spice into a bowl. Add the eggs and beat until smooth.

3 Reserve 25 g/1 oz of the chopped nuts, 40 g/1½ oz of the chopped chocolate and half the glacé ginger. Add the remainder to the bowl with the mixed dried fruit and stir until evenly combined.

4 Turn the mixture into the prepared tin and level the surface. Scatter with the reserved nuts, chocolate and ginger.

5 Bake in a preheated oven, 150°C (300°F), Gas Mark 2, for 1¼–1½ hours until a skewer inserted into the centre comes out clean. Leave to cool in the tin.

Serves 12–14

Preparation time: 20 minutes

Cooking time: 1¼–1½ hours

Oven temperature: 150°C (300°F), Gas Mark 2

56

Chocolate Eclairs

PASTRY:
- 60 g/2½ oz plain flour
- 50 g/2 oz lightly salted butter
- 150 ml/¼ pint cold water
- 2 eggs, beaten

TO FINISH:
- 300 ml/½ pint double cream
- 1 tablespoon icing sugar
- 125 g/4 oz plain chocolate, broken into pieces
- 40 g/1½ oz white chocolate, broken into pieces

1 Make the pastry. Sift the flour on to greaseproof paper. Put the butter in a small saucepan with the water and heat gently until the butter melts.
2 Bring to the boil and remove from the heat. Immediately tip in the flour and beat until the mixture forms a ball which comes away from the sides of the pan. Leave to cool for 3 minutes.
3 Gradually beat the eggs into the dough, a little at a time, until glossy.
4 Lightly grease, then dampen a large baking sheet. Put the pastry in a large piping bag fitted with a 1 cm/½ inch plain nozzle.
5 Pipe 7.5 cm/3 inch fingers on to the baking sheet. Alternatively, use a teaspoon to place similar-sized lengths of dough on the baking sheet.

6 Bake in a preheated oven, 200°C (400°F), Gas Mark 6, for about 35 minutes until well risen, crisp and golden. Make a slit down the side of each bun to release the steam, then transfer to a wire rack to cool.
7 Whip the cream with the icing sugar until just peaking. Spoon or pipe into the éclairs.
8 Melt the plain and white chocolates in separate bowls over saucepans of simmering water. Spread a little plain chocolate over each bun, then spoon a little white chocolate over the centre of each, swirling into the plain with a spoon or cocktail stick. Leave the chocolate to set lightly before serving.

Makes about 14
Preparation time: 25 minutes, plus cooling
Cooking time: about 35 minutes
Oven temperature: 200°C (400°F), Gas Mark 6

VARIATION

Chocolate Profiteroles

Make the dough as left and spoon or pipe 2.5 cm/1 inch rounds on to the prepared baking sheet. Bake as above and make a hole in the side of each bun to allow the steam to escape. Return the buns to the oven for 2 minutes to dry out. Cool, then fill with whipped cream. Pile on to a serving plate. Serve the profiteroles with Glossy Chocolate Sauce (see page 8).

Fruit and Nut Chocolate Fingers

The combination of dried fruit, nuts and seeds is always a delicious one. But add chocolate to the mixture and the result is unbeatable.

- 250 g/8 oz unsalted butter or margarine
- 250 g/8 oz caster sugar
- 175 g/6 oz golden syrup
- 150 g/5 oz dried apricots, roughly chopped
- 75 g/3 oz chopped mixed nuts, such as walnuts or pecans, hazelnuts, almonds and Brazil nuts
- 50 g/2 oz sunflower seeds
- 175 g/6 oz plain or milk chocolate polka dots
- 425 g/14 oz porridge oats

1 Grease a shallow rectangular Swiss roll tin, measuring about 30 x 23 cm/12 x 9 inches, ensuring the corners are well greased.
2 Put the butter or margarine in a saucepan with the sugar and syrup, and heat gently until the butter has melted. Remove from the heat and leave to cool.
3 Put the roughly chopped apricots, the mixed nuts, sunflower seeds, chocolate polka dots and porridge oats in a large bowl. Add the melted butter and syrup mixture, and stir well until all the ingredients are evenly combined together.
4 Turn into the prepared tin, pushing the mixture gently into the corners, and bake in a preheated oven, 180°C (350°F), Gas Mark 4, for 30 minutes or until the mixture is golden around the edges.
5 Leave the baked mixture in the tin until it is almost cold, then turn out on to a board and cut it into fingers. Store in an airtight tin.

Makes about 24
Preparation time: 10 minutes, plus cooling
Cooking time: about 30 minutes
Oven temperature: 180°C (350°F), Gas Mark 4

Chocolate Teabread with Spiced Butter

This is a traditional teabread with a difference – cocoa powder is added.

- 300 g/10 oz dried fruit salad
- 300 ml/½ pint cold tea
- 175 g/6 oz caster sugar
- 200 g/7 oz self-raising flour
- 50 g/2 oz cocoa powder
- ½ teaspoon bicarbonate of soda
- 1 egg

SPICED BUTTER:
- 125 g/4 oz unsalted butter, softened
- 2 tablespoons icing sugar
- 1 teaspoon ground mixed spice

1 Grease and line the base and long sides of a 1 kg/2 lb loaf tin. Blend the dried fruit salad in a food processor until chopped into small chunks.

2 Transfer the fruit to a small saucepan and add the tea and sugar. Bring to the boil, remove from the heat and leave to cool completely.

3 Sift the flour, cocoa powder and bicarbonate of soda into a large bowl. Add the egg and the fruit mixture, including any liquid, and mix until evenly combined.

4 Turn into the prepared tin and level the surface. Bake in a preheated oven, 180°C (350°F), Gas Mark 4, for about 1¼ hours until a skewer, inserted into the centre, comes out clean.

5 Meanwhile, make the spiced butter. Beat together all the ingredients in a bowl until smooth and creamy. Transfer to a small serving dish.

6 Leave the cake to cool in the tin for 10 minutes, then transfer to a wire rack to cool completely. Serve in slices with the spiced butter.

Makes 10 slices

Preparation time: 20 minutes, plus cooling
Cooking time: about 1¼ hours
Oven temperature: 180°C (350°F), Gas Mark 4

Chocolate Pecan Slice

The pecan nuts give an interesting variation in texture to this delicious cake. In addition, lemon juice and maple syrup add an exciting combination of flavours.

- 175 g/6 oz unsalted butter or margarine, softened
- 175 g/6 oz light muscovado sugar
- grated rind of 1 lemon
- 250 g/8 oz self-raising flour
- ½ teaspoon baking powder
- 2 eggs
- 1 tablespoon milk
- 175 g/6 oz white chocolate, chopped
- 100 g/3½ oz pecan halves

GLAZE:
- 5 tablespoons maple syrup
- ½ teaspoon cornflour
- 2 tablespoons cold water
- 2 tablespoons lemon juice

1 Grease and line the base of a shallow 23 cm/9 inch square baking tin.
2 Put the butter or margarine, sugar and lemon rind in a large bowl. Sift the flour and baking powder into the bowl.
3 Add the eggs and beat until light and creamy. Stir in the milk, then the chopped chocolate and turn into the prepared tin. Level the surface.
4 Scatter with the pecan halves and bake in a preheated oven, 180°C (350°F), Gas Mark 4, for 40–45 minutes or until the centre feels firm.
5 Make the glaze. Drizzle the cake with 3 tablespoons of the maple syrup.

Blend the cornflour in a small saucepan with the water. Stir in the lemon juice and remaining maple syrup. Bring to the boil, stirring constantly, then leave to cool for 5 minutes. Spoon or brush over the cake. Serve cut into rectangles.

Serves 12
Preparation time: 20 minutes
Cooking time: about 45 minutes
Oven temperature: 180°C (350°F), Gas Mark 4

Rich Chocolate Slice

This cake, rich and dark, is every chocoholic's dream.

- 175 g/6 oz plain chocolate, broken into pieces
- 125 g/4 oz unsalted butter or margarine, softened
- 125 g/4 oz caster sugar
- 200 g/7 oz ground hazelnuts
- 4 eggs, separated

TO FINISH:
- 125 g/4 oz plain chocolate, broken into pieces
- 25 g/1 oz unsalted butter
- roughly chopped toasted hazelnuts

1 Line the base and sides of a 35 x 10 cm/14 x 4 inch loose-bottomed, rectangular flan tin. (Alternatively, you can use a 20 cm/8 inch square shallow tin.)
2 Put the chocolate in a heatproof bowl and leave over a saucepan of simmering water until melted.
3 Cream together the butter or margarine and sugar until pale and fluffy. Stir in the ground hazelnuts, egg yolks and melted chocolate.
4 Whisk the egg whites until stiff. Using a large metal spoon, fold a quarter of the whites into the chocolate mixture, then fold in the remainder.
5 Turn into the prepared tin and bake in a preheated oven, 180°C (350°F), Gas Mark 4, for about 50 minutes until just firm. Remove from the oven and allow to cool. (The cake might sink slightly in the centre because of the lightness of the mixture.)
6 To finish the cake, put the chocolate in a heatproof bowl with the butter and melt over a pan of simmering water. Stir lightly.
7 Remove the cake from the tin and spread with the chocolate mixture, letting it run down the sides. Scatter with the hazelnuts.

Serves 10
Preparation time: 25 minutes, plus cooling
Cooking time: about 50 minutes
Oven temperature: 180°C (350°F), Gas Mark 4

VARIATION

Rich Chocolate Cake with White Chocolate Glaze

Make the cake as above and leave to cool. Finely chop 125 g/4 oz white chocolate. Bring 75 ml/3 fl oz double cream to the boil in a small saucepan. Remove from the heat and stir in the chocolate. Leave until the chocolate has melted, then stir gently. Spoon over the cake.

Rippled Chocolate and Banana Teabread

- 200 g/7 oz plain chocolate, broken into pieces
- ½ teaspoon ground ginger
- 200 g/7 oz unsalted butter or margarine, softened
- 2 ripe bananas
- 175 g/6 oz caster sugar
- 3 eggs
- 250 g/8 oz self-raising flour
- ½ teaspoon baking powder
- 50 g/2 oz plain chocolate, chopped, to decorate
- icing sugar, for dusting (optional)

1 Lightly grease the base and long sides of a 1 kg/2 lb loaf tin. Put the chocolate in a heatproof bowl with the ginger and 25 g/1 oz of the butter or margarine. Leave over a saucepan of simmering water until melted.

2 Mash the bananas. Put the remaining butter or margarine in a bowl with the sugar and beat until the mixture is creamy.

3 Add all the eggs and the banana purée. Sift the flour and baking powder into the bowl. Beat together until smooth.

4 Spread a quarter of the creamed mixture into the tin, then spoon over a third of the chocolate mixture. Spread with another quarter of the cake mixture, then more chocolate. Repeat the layering, finishing with a layer of the cake mixture.

5 Scatter the chopped chocolate down the centre of the cake. Bake in a preheated oven, 180°C (350°F), Gas Mark 4, for about 1 hour until a skewer inserted into the centre comes out clean. Leave in the tin for 10 minutes before transferring to a wire rack to cool completely. Dust with icing sugar, if liked.

Makes 10 slices
Preparation time: 20 minutes
Cooking time: about 1 hour
Oven temperature: 180°C (350°F), Gas Mark 4

3 Divide the dough into 8 even-sized pieces. Roll out each piece on a lightly floured surface to a round, about 10 cm/4 inches in diameter.

4 Place a spoonful of the chocolate mixture in the centre. Bring the edges of the dough up around the chocolate and pinch together firmly to seal in the chocolate. Place on a lightly greased baking sheet and shape the remaining pieces of dough in the same way.

5 Cover with oiled clingfilm and leave to rise for 30 minutes. Mix together the caster sugar and cinnamon on a large plate.

6 Heat a 5 cm/2 inch depth of oil in a large saucepan to 180–190°C (350–375°F) or until a cube of bread browns in 30 seconds.

7 Slide half the doughnuts, one at a time, from the baking sheet on to an oiled fish slice and add to the oil. Fry for about 3 minutes until puffed and golden, turning down the heat if the oil bubbles too furiously.

8 Drain the doughnuts on kitchen paper and toss in the spiced sugar. Cook the remaining doughnuts in the same way.

Makes 8

Preparation time: 20 minutes, plus rising
Cooking time: about 6 minutes

Spiced Chocolate Doughnuts

Freshly baked doughnuts are impossible to resist. Serve warm, when the milk chocolate filling will be meltingly good!

- 285 g/9½ oz packet bread mix
- ¼ teaspoon ground nutmeg
- ½ teaspoon ground cinnamon
- 15 g/½ oz caster sugar
- 150 g/5 oz milk chocolate, broken into pieces
- 20 g/¾ oz unsalted butter

TO FINISH:
- 50 g/2 oz caster sugar
- 1 teaspoon ground cinnamon
- oil, for deep frying

1 Put the bread mix, spices and sugar in a bowl and make up with milk or water, following the directions on the bread mix packet. Knead the dough and put in a bowl. Cover the bowl with clingfilm and leave the dough to rise until doubled in size.

2 Put the chocolate and butter in a heatproof bowl and leave over a pan of simmering water until the chocolate has melted. Stir lightly.

Double Chocolate Brownies

These versions of this popular cake are made with a mixture of white and plain chocolate – double chocolate and delicious.

- 375 g/12 oz white chocolate
- 50 g/2 oz unsalted butter
- 250 g/8 oz plain chocolate
- 3 eggs
- 150 g/5 oz caster sugar
- 175 g/6 oz self-raising flour
- 1 teaspoon almond essence
- 150 g/5 oz broken walnuts

1 Grease and line a 28 x 20 cm/11 x 8 inch shallow baking tin with greaseproof paper. Break up 125 g/4 oz of the white chocolate and put in a heatproof bowl with the butter. Leave over a saucepan of simmering water until melted. Stir lightly.

2 Roughly chop the remaining white and plain chocolate.

3 Whisk the eggs and sugar together in a large bowl until foamy. Beat in the melted chocolate mixture. Sift the flour into the bowl and stir it into the mixture with the almond essence, walnuts and chopped white and plain chocolate.

4 Turn the brownie mixture into the prepared tin and bake in a preheated oven, 190°C (375°F), Gas Mark 5, for 35 minutes until risen and just firm. Leave the baked mixture in the tin to cool.

5 When cool, turn out of the tin on to a board and cut into the traditional brownie squares and rectangles.

Makes 14–16
Preparation time: 20 minutes
Cooking time: 35 minutes
Oven temperature: 190°C (375°F), Gas Mark 5

VARIATION

Dark Chocolate Brownies

Use all plain chocolate and roughly chop 500 g/1 lb. Continue as left, using 250 g/8 oz butter or margarine and 125 g/4 oz self-raising flour.

Chocolate Chip Muffins

There is something comforting about these delicious chocolate muffins with crunchy chocolate chips. An exciting alternative, given as a variation here, is to replace some of the chocolate with pieces of dried banana.

- 175 g/6 oz plain chocolate, broken into pieces
- 350 ml/12 fl oz milk
- 60 g/2½ oz unsalted butter
- 375 g/12 oz self-raising flour
- 1 tablespoon baking powder
- 60 g/2½ oz cocoa powder
- 100 g/3½ oz caster sugar
- 100 g/3½ oz milk chocolate polka dots
- 100 g/3½ oz white chocolate polka dots
- 2 teaspoons vanilla essence
- 1 egg
- 1 egg yolk
- icing sugar, for dusting

1 Line sections of a muffin tin with paper muffin cases. Put the chocolate in a small heavy-based saucepan with half the milk and the butter. Heat gently until the chocolate has melted. Leave to cool.
2 Sift the flour, baking powder and cocoa powder into a bowl. Stir in the sugar and polka dots.
3 Beat the remaining milk with the vanilla essence, egg and egg yolk, and add to the bowl with the chocolate mixture. Using a large metal spoon, fold the ingredients together until only just combined.

4 Spoon the mixture into the paper cases until almost filled. Bake in a preheated oven, 220°C (425°F), Gas Mark 7, for 25 minutes or until well risen and just firm. Transfer to a wire rack to cool. Serve the muffins dusted with icing sugar.

Makes 12
Preparation time: 15 minutes, plus cooling
Cooking time: about 25 minutes
Oven temperature: 220°C (425°F), Gas Mark 7

VARIATION

Chocolate and Banana Muffins

Finely chop 125 g/4 oz dried banana and use instead of the plain chocolate polka dots.

Chocolate Ginger Parkin

Chocolate and ginger combine with treacle and syrup to make this delicious cake, perfect for cheering up a cold winter's day.

- 250 g/8 oz black treacle
- 250 g/8 oz golden syrup
- 125 g/4 oz unsalted butter or margarine
- 375 g/12 oz plain flour
- 75 g/3 oz cocoa powder
- 2 teaspoons ground mixed spice
- 75 g/3 oz light muscovado sugar
- 375 g/12 oz medium oatmeal
- 300 ml/½ pint milk
- 1 egg
- ½ teaspoon bicarbonate of soda
- 250 g/8 oz milk chocolate, roughly chopped
- 2 tablespoons porridge oats

1 Grease and line a 20 cm/8 inch square cake tin. Put the treacle, syrup and butter or margarine in a saucepan and heat gently until the butter has melted. Remove from the heat and leave to cool.
2 Sift the flour, cocoa powder and spice into a large bowl. Stir in the sugar and oatmeal.
3 Mix together the milk, egg and bicarbonate of soda, and add to the bowl with the melted mixture and the chopped chocolate. Stir lightly until the ingredients are combined.
4 Turn into the prepared tin and scatter with the porridge oats. Bake in a preheated oven, 180°C (350°F), Gas Mark 4, for about 1¼ hours until the crust is cracked and a skewer, inserted into the centre, comes out clean.
5 Leave to cool in the tin. Cut into squares to serve. Store in an airtight container for 1–2 weeks.

Makes 16–20 squares
Preparation time: 20 minutes
Cooking time: about 1¼ hours
Oven temperature: 180°C (350°F),
Gas Mark 4

Chocolate Fudge Cake

For complete indulgence, serve this classic favourite after a meal with plenty of single cream.

CAKE:
- 250 ml/8 fl oz milk
- 1 tablespoon lemon juice
- 125 g/4 oz plain chocolate, broken into pieces
- 125 g/4 oz unsalted butter or margarine
- 250 g/8 oz caster sugar
- 2 eggs
- 300 g/10 oz self-raising flour
- 1 teaspoon bicarbonate of soda
- 2 tablespoons cocoa powder

FILLING:
- 150 ml/¼ pint double cream
- 1 quantity Almond Praline (see page 8)

ICING:
- 250 g/8 oz plain chocolate, broken into pieces
- 125 g/4 oz unsalted butter
- 200 g/7 oz icing sugar
- 5 tablespoons milk
- chocolate caraque, to decorate (see page 7)
- icing sugar, for dusting

1 Grease and line a 20 cm/8 inch round cake tin. Mix together the milk and lemon juice. Put the chocolate in a heatproof bowl and leave over a saucepan of gently simmering water until it has melted.

2 Beat together the butter or margarine and sugar to soften, in a large bowl. Add the eggs and beat in. Sift the flour, bicarbonate of soda and cocoa powder into the bowl and mix well.

3 Add half the soured milk and beat well. Stir in the melted chocolate and remaining milk and beat until smooth. Turn into the prepared tin and level the surface.

4 Bake in a preheated oven, 160°C (325°F), Gas Mark 3, for 1¼-1½ hours or until well risen and a skewer, inserted into the centre, comes out clean. Leave to cool in the tin.

5 Split the cake horizontally into 3 layers. Lightly whip the cream and stir in the praline. Use to sandwich the layers of cake together. Place on a serving plate.

6 Make the icing. Put the chocolate in a heatproof bowl with the butter and leave over a saucepan of simmering water until melted. Stir once. Remove from the heat.

7 Add the icing sugar and milk, and beat until smooth. Leave the icing until cool enough to hold its shape.

8 Using a palette knife, spread the icing all over the top and sides of the cake. Scatter with chocolate caraque and serve dusted with icing sugar.

Serves 14–16

Preparation time: 45 minutes, plus cooling
Cooking time: 1¼-1½ hours
Oven temperature: 160°C (325°F) Gas Mark 3

Biscuits and Cookies

Brandy Snap Waves

75 g/3 oz plain flour

1 teaspoon ground ginger

75 g/3 oz unsalted butter

75 g/3 oz caster sugar

3 tablespoons golden syrup

2 tablespoons brandy

75 g/3 oz plain or bitter chocolate, broken into pieces

1 Line 2 baking sheets with non-stick greaseproof paper. Arrange 3 wooden spoons on a work surface, parallel to each other with a 1 cm/½ inch space between each.

2 Sift the flour and ginger on to greaseproof paper. Heat the butter, sugar and syrup in a saucepan until the butter dissolves. Remove from the heat and stir in the flour, ginger and brandy. Mix to a smooth paste.

3 Place 3 dessertspoonfuls of the mixture, spaced well apart, on to one baking sheet and bake in a preheated oven, 190°C (375°F), Gas Mark 5, for 6–8 minutes until the biscuits have spread to a lacy texture. Remove from the oven, leave for a few seconds, then lift the biscuits with a palette knife. Drape over spoons, pressing down between them.

4 Shape the other brandy snaps in the same way. (If they've hardened before you have shaped them, pop the biscuits back in the oven for a few seconds to soften them.)

5 Bake the remaining mixture on the second baking sheet while shaping the first.

6 Put the chocolate in a heatproof bowl over a pan of simmering water to melt. Dip the edges of the biscuits in the chocolate and leave to set on a greaseproof-lined tray.

Makes about 15

Preparation time: 25 minutes

Cooking time: 6–8 minutes each batch

Oven temperature: 190°C (375 °F), Gas Mark 5

Chocolate Pistachio Biscotti

Colourful pistachios and dark chocolate are used to flavour these crisp Italian biscuits. They're traditionally served after dinner, dipped in Vino Santo, which is a sweet dessert wine. If you buy shelled pistachio nuts ensure they are within their 'use by' date.

- 175 g/6 oz plain chocolate, broken into pieces
- 25 g/1 oz lightly salted butter
- 200 g/7 oz self-raising flour
- 1½ teaspoons baking powder
- 75 g/3 oz caster sugar
- 50 g/2 oz polenta
- finely grated rind of 1 lemon
- 2 teaspoons brandy
- 1 egg, lightly beaten
- 75 g/3 oz pistachio nuts
- icing sugar, for dusting

1 Lightly grease a baking sheet. Put the chocolate in a heatproof bowl with the butter and heat over a pan of simmering water until the chocolate has melted. Remove from the heat and cool slightly.

2 Sift the flour and baking powder into a bowl. Add the sugar, polenta, lemon rind, brandy, egg and pistachio nuts.

3 Add the chocolate mixture and mix to make a soft dough. Divide the mixture in half. Using lightly floured hands, shape each half into a sausage, about 28 cm/11 inches long.

4 Transfer to the prepared baking sheet and flatten the dough until about 2 cm/¾ inch thick. Bake in a preheated oven, 160°C (325°F), Gas Mark 3, for 30 minutes until risen and firm.

5 Leave to cool, then cut each piece diagonally into thin biscuits. Return to the baking sheet, spacing them slightly apart, and bake for a further 10 minutes or until crisp.

6 Transfer to a wire rack to cool. Dust with icing sugar and store in an airtight tin for up to 1 week.

Makes about 24

Preparation time: 20 minutes, plus cooling
Cooking time: 40 minutes
Oven temperature: 160°C (325°F), Gas Mark 3

1 Lightly grease 2 baking sheets. Beat together the butter and sugar until pale and creamy. Add the egg, flour, baking powder and oats, and beat until well combined.

2 Stir in the chocolate and peanuts. Using a dessertspoon, place spoonfuls of the mixture, spaced slightly apart, on the baking sheets. Flatten slightly with a fork.

3 Bake in a preheated oven, 180°C (350°F), Gas Mark 4, for 15–20 minutes until spread and turning pale golden brown.

4 Leave the cookies on the baking sheets for 2 minutes, then transfer to a wire rack to cool. Serve dusted with icing sugar, if liked.

Makes about 28

Preparation time: 15 minutes
Cooking time: 15–20 minutes
Oven temperature: 180°C (350°F), Gas Mark 4

Chunky Chocolate Nut Cookies

Generous chunks of chopped chocolate and a handful of peanuts give these buttery cookies an unbeatable flavour. Use milk or white chocolate, or use nuts other than peanuts for different but equally delicious results.

- 125 g/4 oz lightly salted butter, softened
- 125 g/4 oz light muscovado sugar
- 1 egg, lightly beaten
- 150 g/5 oz plain flour, sifted
- ½ teaspoon baking powder
- 75 g/3 oz porridge oats
- 200 g/7 oz plain chocolate, roughly chopped
- 50 g/2 oz unsalted peanuts, roughly chopped
- icing sugar, for dusting (optional)

Chocolate Palmiers

- 25 g/1 oz plain chocolate
- 50 g/2 oz caster sugar
- 250 g/8 oz puff pastry
- beaten egg, to glaze
- caster sugar, to serve

1 Lightly grease 2 baking sheets. Grate the chocolate and mix with 25 g/1 oz of the caster sugar.
2 Roll out the pastry on a lightly floured surface to a 20 cm/8 inch square and sprinkle with the remaining sugar.
3 Continue rolling the pastry until the square measures about 28 cm/11 inches across. Brush with beaten egg and sprinkle with the chocolate mixture.
4 Roll up the pastry from one side to the centre, then roll up the other side so the 2 rolls meet. Brush the points where the rolls meet with a little beaten egg.
5 Using a sharp knife, cut across the rolls into thin slices. Roll the slices very lightly to flatten and place on the prepared baking sheets.
6 Bake in a preheated oven, 220°C (425°F), Gas Mark 7, for about 10 minutes until golden. Transfer to a wire rack to cool. Sprinkle with caster sugar.

Makes about 24
Preparation time: 10 minutes
Cooking time: about 10 minutes
Oven temperature: 220°C (425°F), Gas Mark 7

VARIATION

Coffee Cream Palmiers

Make the palmiers as above and leave to cool. Dissolve 1 tablespoonful of coffee granules in 2 tablespoons hot water. Place in a bowl with 150 ml/¼ pint double cream and 1 tablespoon icing sugar. Add 1 tablespoon Tia Maria or other coffee flavoured liqueur, if liked, and whip the cream until just peaking. Use the cream to sandwich the palmiers together in pairs.

Millionaire's Fingers

Millionaire's Fingers are a chocolate version of the classic caramel-covered shortbread squares. Let them set completely before you coat them in melted chocolate.

SHORTBREAD:
- 75 g/3 oz unsalted butter or margarine, softened
- 40 g/1½ oz light muscovado sugar
- 75 g/3 oz plain flour, sifted
- 25 g/1 oz cornflour

TO FINISH:
- 250 g/8 oz condensed milk
- 50 g/2 oz caster sugar
- 75 g/3 oz unsalted butter
- 2 tablespoons golden syrup
- 250 g/8 oz plain chocolate, broken into pieces

1 Grease and line the base and sides of an 18 cm/7 inch square shallow baking tin or cake tin.
2 Beat the butter or margarine and sugar in a bowl until light and fluffy. Add the flours and beat to form a soft dough. Knead lightly and turn into the prepared tin, levelling the surface with the fingers.
3 Bake in a preheated oven, 180°C (350°F), Gas Mark 4, for 25 minutes or until a pale golden colour. Leave to cool in the tin.
4 Put the condensed milk, sugar, butter and syrup in a small heavy-based saucepan and heat gently until the sugar dissolves. Bring to the boil, then simmer very gently, stirring, for about 5 minutes until thickened and like pale fudge in colour.
5 Pour over the shortbread base and leave to cool.
6 Once completely cooled, remove from the tin and cut in half. Cut each half into 10 fingers. Space slightly apart on a greaseproof lined tray.
7 Put the chocolate in a heatproof bowl and leave over a pan of simmering water until melted.
8 Using a teaspoon, spoon the melted chocolate over the fingers, easing it around the sides with the back of the spoon until the bars are mostly covered. Touch the tops of the fingers with the back of the spoon to texture the surface. Leave to set.

Makes 20
Preparation time: 30 minutes, plus cooling
Cooking time: about 30 minutes
Oven temperature: 180°C (350°F), Gas Mark 4

Scribbled Chocolate Florentines

- 50 g/2 oz flaked almonds
- 25 g/1 oz glacé cherries
- 60 g/2½ oz unsalted butter
- 50 g/2 oz caster sugar
- 2 tablespoons double cream
- 25 g/1 oz pumpkin or sunflower seeds
- 25 g/1 oz raisins
- 2 tablespoons plain flour
- 125 g/4 oz plain chocolate, broken into pieces

1 Lightly grease a large baking sheet. Lightly crush the flaked almonds. Roughly chop the cherries.

2 Melt the butter in a saucepan. Stir in the sugar until dissolved, then bring to the boil. Remove from the heat and beat in the cream, seeds, raisins, cherries, almonds and flour.

3 Place heaped teaspoonsful of the mixture, spaced well apart, on the prepared baking sheet. (You'll need to bake in 2 batches.)

4 Bake in a preheated oven, 180°C (350°F), Gas Mark 4, for about 8 minutes, until the biscuits have spread and the edges are turning dark golden.

5 Using a large oiled plain metal biscuit cutter, push the edges of each biscuit into the centre to give neat edges. Return the biscuits to the oven for a further 2 minutes.

6 Transfer the florentines to a wire rack to cool and cook the remaining mixture in the same way.

7 Put the chocolate in a heatproof bowl over a saucepan of simmering water and leave until melted. Place the chocolate in a piping bag fitted with a writing nozzle. (Alternatively, use a paper piping bag and snip off the tip.)

8 Pipe scribbled lines all over one side of the biscuits and leave on the wire rack until the chocolate has set.

Makes about 14

Preparation time: 20 minutes, plus cooling
Cooking time: about 12 minutes
Oven temperature: 180°C (350°F), Gas Mark 4

Chocolate Tuiles

These delicate biscuits are good with coffee or served with a creamy dessert.

- **15 g/½ oz flaked almonds**
- **25 g/1 oz unsalted butter**
- **3 egg whites**
- **100 g/3½ oz caster sugar**
- **2 tablespoons plain flour**
- **1 tablespoon cocoa powder**
- **2 tablespoons double cream**
- **icing sugar, for dusting**

1 Line 2 baking sheets with non-stick greaseproof parchment. Lightly crush the almonds between the fingers. Melt the butter and cool slightly.
2 Lightly whisk the egg whites and sugar. Sift the flour and cocoa powder into the bowl. Add the cream, melted butter and almonds, and mix together.
3 Place 8 teaspoonsful of the mixture, spaced well apart, on one baking sheet and bake in a preheated oven, 180°C (350°F), Gas Mark 4, for 6–8 minutes until the edges are turning dark golden.
4 Remove from the oven and leave for 30 seconds. Carefully lift the biscuits on to a rolling pin and leave for about 15 seconds until set into curved shapes. (If some of the biscuits have hardened before you've had time to shape them, put them back in the oven for a few seconds to soften them.)
5 Cook the remaining mixture in the same way, using the second baking sheet to cook more biscuits while shaping the first.
6 Store in an airtight container for 3–4 days and serve dusted with icing sugar.

Makes about 24
Preparation time: 15 minutes
Cooking time: 6–8 minutes each batch
Oven temperature: 180°C (350°F), Gas Mark 4

VARIATION

Chocolate Hazelnut Cigars

Make the paste as above, using 15 g/½ oz chopped and toasted hazelnuts instead of the almonds. Place 3 dessertspoonsful of the mixture, spaced well apart, on the greaseproof paper-lined baking sheet and bake as above. Cool for 1 minute, then lift one biscuit and wrap loosely around the handle of a wooden spoon until set in shape. Twist away from the handle and shape the remainder in the same way.

Chocolate Layer Biscuits

Chocolate Layer Biscuits look as pretty as they are good to eat.

- 175 g/6 oz unsalted butter or margarine, softened
- 75 g/3 oz icing sugar
- 1 teaspoon vanilla essence
- 275 g/9 oz plain flour
- 2 tablespoons cocoa powder
- beaten egg white, to glaze
- 125 g/4 oz plain chocolate, broken into pieces

1 Lightly grease a large baking sheet. Beat the butter or margarine and icing sugar in a bowl until light and fluffy. Add the vanilla essence.
2 Sift the flour into the bowl and beat until the ingredients start to bind. Transfer half the mixture to another bowl and stir in the cocoa. Knead the 2 mixtures into doughs. Wrap separately and chill for 30 minutes.
3 Roll out each dough on a lightly floured surface to a 25 x 15 cm/10 x 6 inch rectangle. Brush the plain dough with egg white and lay the cocoa-flavoured dough over it. Brush with more egg white.

4 Trim the edges, then cut lengthways into 6 strips. Stack the strips on top of each other to make layers. Cut across into thin slices and place on the baking sheet, striped sides facing up.
5 Bake in a preheated oven, 180°C (350°F), Gas Mark 4, for about 10 minutes until just beginning to colour. Leave the biscuits on the baking sheet for 2 minutes, then transfer to a wire rack to cool.
6 Put the chocolate in a heatproof bowl and leave over a saucepan of simmering water until melted. Half dip the biscuits in the melted chocolate, letting the excess drip back into the bowl. Place on a sheet of greaseproof paper and leave to set.

Makes 20
Preparation time: 25 minutes, plus cooling
Cooking time: about 10 minutes
Oven temperature: 180°C (350°F), Gas Mark 4

VARIATION

Chocolate Ring Biscuits

Make the doughs as above and thinly roll each. Using a 6 cm/2½ inch and 2.5 cm/1 inch biscuit cutter, cut out rings from the doughs, carefully removing the central circle. Transfer the rings to the baking sheet and re-position the centres to alternate the colours. Bake as above, then roll the edges of the biscuits in melted chocolate.

Chocolate Spice Puffs

Because these biscuits are pastry-based, they won't keep for more than a day or two.

- 2 teaspoons cocoa powder
- ¼ teaspoon ground mixed spice
- 2 tablespoons caster sugar
- 250 g/8 oz puff pastry
- beaten egg, to glaze
- 125 g/4 oz plain chocolate, broken into pieces
- 2 tablespoons apricot jam
- 1 tablespoon lemon juice

1 Lightly grease a large baking sheet. Mix together the cocoa powder, spice and 1 tablespoon of the sugar.
2 Thinly roll out the pastry on a lightly floured surface to a 35 x 25 cm/14 x 10 inch rectangle. Cut the pastry in half and brush each half with beaten egg. Scatter one half with the cocoa mixture and cover with the other piece of pastry.
3 Roll the pastry lightly until firmly sandwiched together and the pastry is about 2 mm/⅛ inch thick.
4 Cut the pastry into 5 cm/2 inch wide strips. Cut diagonally across each strip to make diamond shapes. Prick with a fork. Brush with beaten egg and sprinkle with the remaining sugar. Transfer to the prepared baking sheet.
5 Bake in a preheated oven, 200°C (400°F), Gas Mark 6, for about 15 minutes until risen and golden. Transfer to a wire rack to cool.

6 Put the chocolate in a heatproof bowl and leave over a saucepan of simmering water until melted. Dip the edges of the biscuits in the chocolate, letting the excess drip back into the bowl. Leave to set on a greaseproof-lined tray.
7 Melt the jam in a small saucepan and press through a sieve into a bowl. Stir in the lemon juice and use to glaze the biscuits lightly.

Makes about 20
Preparation time: 20 minutes, plus cooling
Cooking time: about 15 minutes
Oven temperature: 200°C (400°F), Gas Mark 6

Confectionery and Sweets

Chocolate Pralines

150 g/5 oz milk chocolate, broken into pieces
3 tablespoons double cream
¼ teaspoon vanilla essence
1 quantity Almond Praline (see page 8)
150 g/5 oz plain chocolate, broken into pieces

1 Dampen a 500 g/1 lb loaf tin and line the base and half way up the sides with non-stick greaseproof paper.
2 Put the milk chocolate in a heatproof bowl with the cream and vanilla essence and leave over a saucepan of simmering water until melted.
3 Remove from the heat and leave to cool slightly. Reserve 1 tablespoon of the praline and stir the remainder into the chocolate. Turn into the prepared tin. Level the surface and chill until firm.
4 Put the plain chocolate in a heatproof bowl over a saucepan of simmering water and leave until melted.
5 Lift the chocolate praline from the tin. Cut lengthways into 4 bars, then cut across into squares. Using a fork, dip the squares into the chocolate, letting the excess drip back into the bowl.
6 Place the coated chocolates on a greaseproof paper-lined tray. Decorate with the reserved crushed praline and leave to set.

Makes 28
Preparation time: 25 minutes

Chocolate Casket

A beautifully shaped box, made entirely of chocolate, makes a clever container for an assortment of homemade chocolates. The decorative lid can be as simple or as elaborate as you wish – the matt sheen of the modelling chocolate looks effective against the rich gloss of the box, but a spray of chocolate leaves or small fresh flowers would look equally good.

- 375 g/12 oz plain chocolate
- white, milk and plain chocolate curls and ribbons (see pages 7–8)
- assortment of homemade chocolates

1 Make templates. Cut out a diamond shape in thin card which measures 20 cm/8 inches between the longest points and 12 cm/5 inches between the shortest points. Cut a rectangle of card which measures the length of one of the sides of the diamond and is 3 cm/1¼ inches wide.

2 Secure a large sheet of acetate or cellophane (available from office stationers) on to a tray. Melt the chocolate, following the directions for Easter Eggs on page 92.

3 Using a palette knife, spread a little chocolate on to the lined tray large enough to fit the diamond-shaped template for the base. Spread another area of the same size to cut a lid.

4 Spread another area of chocolate large enough to cut out 4 rectangular templates for the sides.

5 Leave the chocolate until dry but not brittle. Lay the diamond template over one piece of chocolate and cut around it, discarding the trimmings. Repeat for the lid. Use the rectangular template to cut out 4 shapes.

6 Cover the chocolate shapes with greaseproof paper and lightly weight with a baking sheet for several hours until the chocolate is brittle.

7 Carefully peel the acetate or cellophane away from the chocolate shapes. Melt a little leftover chocolate and pipe it around the edges of the diamond base. Position the rectangular shapes around the sides with the shiny sides facing outwards. Pipe a little more chocolate inside the box where the rectangles meet to strengthen the joins.

8 Spread a little melted chocolate on to the centre of the lid and position the decorations. Arrange the homemade chocolates inside the casket and position the lid.

Makes 1 casket

Preparation time: about 45 minutes

Mint Chocolate Meringues

This delicious concoction is certainly something different to do with your after-dinner mints!

- **1 egg white**
- **50 g/2 oz caster sugar**
- **125 g/4 oz plain chocolate after-dinner mints (not soft centres)**
- **25 g/1 oz plain chocolate, broken into pieces**

1 Line a baking sheet with non-stick greaseproof paper. Whisk the egg white in a bowl until stiff. Gradually whisk in the sugar, a little at a time, until the meringue is stiff and glossy.
2 Using 2 teaspoons, pile small mounds of the meringue on the prepared baking sheet, shaping small peaks with the back of a spoon.
3 Bake in a preheated oven, 120°C (250°F), Gas Mark ½, for about 50 minutes until crisp. Leave to cool on the paper.
4 Put the mint chocolates in a heatproof bowl with the plain chocolate and leave over a saucepan of simmering water until melted.
5 Half dip the meringues in the melted chocolate and place on a greaseproof paper-lined tray to set.

Makes about 24
Preparation time: 15 minutes
Cooking time: about 50 minutes
Oven temperature: 120°C (250°F), Gas Mark ½

Rocky Roads

- 125 g/4 oz plain or milk chocolate, broken into pieces
- 25 g/1 oz unsalted butter
- 25 g/1 oz unsalted peanuts
- 25 g/1 oz raisins
- 50 g/2 oz mini marshmallows (or ordinary marshmallows, chopped)

TO DECORATE:

- 50 g/2 oz white chocolate, broken into pieces
- 50 g/2 oz flaked almonds, toasted

1 Put the plain or milk chocolate and butter in a heatproof bowl over a saucepan of simmering water and leave until melted.

2 Stir lightly, then add the peanuts, raisins and marshmallows, and stir gently until coated.

3 Turn out on to a sheet of greaseproof paper and wrap the paper around the mixture, pressing it into a 4 cm/ 1½ inch thick roll. Chill until firm.

4 Put the broken white chocolate into a heatproof bowl and place over a saucepan of simmering water, leave until melted.

5 Unwrap the roll. Scatter the almonds over a clean sheet of greaseproof paper. Working quickly, spread the chocolate roll with the white chocolate, then coat in the flaked almonds.

6 Chill until firm and serve cut into thin slices.

Makes about 30
Preparation time: 25 minutes, plus chilling

Chocolate Marzipan Twists

- 125 g/4 oz ground almonds
- 50 g/2 oz caster sugar
- 50 g/2 oz icing sugar
- 1 tablespoon cocoa powder
- 1 egg white
- 2–3 teaspoons lemon juice
- 50 g/2 oz milk chocolate, broken into pieces

1 Mix together half the almonds and sugars in one bowl and half in another. Stir the cocoa into the second bowl.
2 Lightly beat the egg white until foamy and divide between the two bowls. Add 1 teaspoon lemon juice to each bowl, then lightly knead each to a dough adding a little more lemon juice if either mixture is too dry.
3 On a work surface lightly dusted with icing sugar, roll out the pastes until each is about 7mm/⅓ inch thick.
4 Arrange the rolls side by side, then twist them together into a rope (cutting them into more manageable lengths first, if preferred). Chill on a greaseproof paper-lined tray for 1 hour.
5 Cut the rope into 2.5 cm/1 inch lengths. Put the chocolate in a heatproof bowl over a saucepan of simmering water and leave to melt.
6 Put in a piping bag fitted with a writing nozzle. (Alternatively use a paper piping bag and snip off the tip.) Pipe lines over the twists. Leave to set.

Makes about 16
Preparation time: 25 minutes

Simple Chocolate Fudge

Use a very dark, rich chocolate to achieve a good flavour in this creamy fudge. If you prefer, half dip the fudge in melted chocolate once firm. Store in an airtight container or jar for up to 2 weeks.

- 250 g/8 oz granulated sugar
- 425 g/14 oz can sweetened condensed milk
- 25 g/1 oz unsalted butter
- 1 teaspoon vanilla essence
- 250 g/8 oz plain chocolate, broken into pieces
- 125 g/4 oz plain or milk chocolate, broken into pieces, to decorate (optional)

1 Grease and line the base and half way up the sides of an 18 cm/7 inch cake tin with non-stick greaseproof paper.

2 Put the sugar in a large heavy-based saucepan with the milk, butter and vanilla essence, and heat gently until the sugar dissolves.

3 Bring to the boil and boil for 5–10 minutes, stirring frequently, until the temperature reaches 115°C (240°F) on a sugar thermometer. (Alternatively, drop a teaspoonful of the mixture in a bowl of iced water. You should be able to roll the mixture into a ball between the fingers.)

4 Remove from the heat and beat in the plain chocolate until melted. Pour into the prepared tin and leave for several hours until set.

5 Remove from the tin and peel away the paper. Cut the fudge into small squares. Leave on a greaseproof paper-lined tray to dry out.

6 If you are decorating the fudge, put the chocolate in a heatproof bowl over a saucepan of simmering water and leave until melted. Holding a piece of fudge between the finger and thumb, dip it into the chocolate to coat the base and 2 mm/ ⅛ inch up the sides. Return to the paper and leave to set.

Makes 50–60
Preparation time: 20 minutes, plus chilling
Cooking time: 5–10 minutes

4 Put the white chocolate in a heatproof bowl and leave over a saucepan of simmering water until melted. Cut the candied orange peel into small slivers.

5 Spoon the melted chocolate over the logs, easing it around the sides. Cut at a diagonal angle into 2.5 cm/1 inch lengths and decorate with the orange slivers. Store in a cool place.

Makes about 30
Preparation time: 25 minutes, plus chilling

Chocolate Orange Logs

- 50 g/2 oz ratafia biscuits
- 125 g/4 oz plain or milk chocolate, broken into pieces
- 4 tablespoons double cream
- 1 tablespoon Cointreau or other orange-flavoured liqueur
- icing sugar for dusting
- 75 g/3 oz white chocolate, broken into pieces
- small piece candied orange peel

1 Put the biscuits in a polythene bag and crush finely by rolling with a rolling pin.

2 Put the chocolate in a heatproof bowl over a saucepan of simmering water and leave until melted. Stir in the cream, orange-flavoured liqueur and crushed biscuits.

3 Chill the mixture until quite firm, then roll into a long sausage, about 1 cm/½ inch wide, on a surface lightly dusted with icing sugar. Cut into manageable sized lengths and transfer to a greaseproof paper-lined tray.

Chocolate Nut Slice

Exceedingly rich, this buttery nut cake is best served with after dinner coffee. Cut the cake into small slices or break it into chunks the size of an individual serving, to reveal the whole nuts. Edible rice paper should be used to line the baking tin because it cannot be peeled off the cake once the cake has been baked.

- edible rice paper
- 375 g/12 oz plain chocolate, broken into pieces
- 175 g/6 oz unsalted butter
- 125 g/4 oz digestive biscuits, chopped into small pieces
- 175 g/6 oz mixture whole nuts e.g. almonds, hazelnuts or Brazil nuts

1 Line the base and 2 cm/¾ inch up the sides of an 18 cm/7 inch square shallow baking tin or cake tin with the rice paper.

2 Put the chocolate and butter in a heatproof bowl over a pan of simmering water, leave until melted.
3 Stir in the biscuits and nuts and turn into the prepared tin. Spread the mixture to fill the tin then chill for several hours or overnight until firm.
4 Remove from the tin and cut or break into small pieces.

Serves 14-16
Preparation time: 15 minutes, plus chilling

Chocolate Ginger Clusters

These simple chocolates are strongly flavoured with crystallized ginger. If a milder flavour is preferred, the ginger could be partly, or entirely, replaced by raisins.

- 175 g/6 oz white chocolate, broken into pieces
- 50 g/2 oz crystallized ginger, chopped
- 100 g/3½ oz blanched almonds, lightly toasted and chopped
- 175 g/6 oz plain chocolate, broken into pieces

1 Put the white chocolate into a heatproof bowl and leave over a saucepan of simmering water until the chocolate has melted.
2 Stir the crystallized ginger and the nuts into the melted chocolate. Place teaspoonfuls of the mixture on a baking sheet lined with greaseproof paper. Chill until firm.
3 Put the plain chocolate into a heatproof bowl over a saucepan of simmering water and leave until the chocolate has melted.
4 Pierce each cluster with a thin skewer or wooden cocktail stick and dip into the melted chocolate, allowing any excess to drip back into the bowl. Place on a clean sheet of greaseproof paper to set.

Makes 20–25
Preparation time: 20 minutes, plus chilling

Fresh Cream Truffles

These velvety truffles may be decorated in a variety of ways.

- 125 ml/4 fl oz double cream
- 250 g/8 oz plain chocolate, finely chopped
- 2 tablespoons Cointreau, brandy, rum or coffee-flavoured liqueur

TO DECORATE:

- 2 tablespoons cocoa powder
- 125 g/4 oz plain chocolate, broken
- 50 g/2 oz milk or white chocolate, broken
- 1 tablespoon slivered almonds, toasted

1 Bring the cream just to the boil in a small heavy-based saucepan. Remove from the heat and stir in the chocolate until melted. Turn into a bowl and stir in the liqueur. Chill until quite firm.
2 Put the cocoa powder on a small plate. Dust the palms of your hands with cocoa powder. Take a teaspoonful of the chocolate mixture and roll it into a ball, about 2 cm/¾ inch in diameter. Roll this in the cocoa powder.
3 Use about a third of the mixture to make more cocoa-coated truffles and place on a greaseproof paper-lined tray.
4 Shape the remaining chocolate mixture into 2 cm/¾ inch balls and chill until very firm.
5 Put the plain and milk or white chocolate in separate heatproof bowls and heat until melted. Using a fork or cocktail stick, dip a few truffles in the melted plain chocolate, allowing the excess to drip back into the bowl.

Transfer to the greaseproof-lined tray.
6 When about two-thirds have been coated, decorate some by lightly touching with the back of a fork to give them texture. Decorate a few more with the slivered almonds.
7 Dip the remaining cream truffles in the melted milk or white chocolate. Put the remaining melted chocolate in 2 separate piping bags fitted with writing nozzles.
8 Decorate the plain truffles with lines or swirls of chocolate in contrasting colours. Chill the truffles for up to 1 week before serving.

Makes about 24
Preparation time: 45 minutes, plus chilling

VARIATION

White Chocolate Pralines

Boil the cream and stir in 150 g/5 oz finely chopped white chocolate. When melted, cool it and stir in a half quantity of Almond Praline (see page 8). Shape and dip in white or plain chocolate as left.

Easter Eggs

Making Easter eggs gives you the flexibility to create original designs and fill them, as you wish, with chocolates or even, smaller eggs. An Easter egg mould is needed in order to create this unique gift. For presentation, pack the eggs in boxes, padded with tissue or simply wrap in cellophane. Creative 'two-tone' finishes can be worked on homemade eggs (see variations below) but a professional looking glossy sheen of a single flavour is really unbeatable. Choose luxury chocolate which produces the best sheen and use a chocolate thermometer to achieve the correct temperature.

- 50 g/2 oz plain, milk or white chocolate (for a 6 cm/2½ inch egg)
- 175 g/6 oz plain, milk or white chocolate (for an 11 cm/4½ inch egg)
- 250 g/8 oz plain milk or white chocolate (for a 15-20 cm/6-8 inch egg)
- chocolate ganache, to decorate (see page 9) (optional)

1 Thoroughly wash and dry the insides of the mould, then polish them by rubbing vigorously with cotton wool.
2 Break up the chocolate and put in a heatproof bowl over a pan of simmering water. Leave until the chocolate has melted and the temperature on a chocolate thermometer reaches 46-49°C (115-120°C) for plain chocolate or 43°C (110°F) for milk and white chocolate.
3 Spoon a little chocolate into one half of the mould and spread it until thinly coated. Invert the mould on to a greaseproof paper-lined tray. Coat the other mould in the same way. Leave in a cool place until set.
4 Use the remaining chocolate to give the moulds 1–2 more coats, then put them aside again to set.
5 Gently tap the eggs out on to the surface to unmould. (If difficult to unmould put the eggs in the fridge for 10 minutes then try again, gently tapping the mould with a spoon.) Trim off any excess chocolate from around the bases.
6 To assemble the egg, carefully transfer one half on to a ramekin dish or small bowl so that it is propped up. (Handle the chocolate as little as possible as they easily mark.)
7 Dot the edges of the egg with a little spare melted chocolate and carefully position the other half. Leave to set.
8 If liked, the join can be covered with a decorative border of ganache. Fit a piping bag with a small star nozzle and fill with chocolate ganache. Pipe over the join. Alternatively, tie a ribbon around the egg.

Makes 1 egg
Preparation time: about 30 minutes, plus cooling

VARIATIONS
Polka Dot Eggs

Melt 25 g/1 oz white chocolate. Put in a piping bag fitted with a writing nozzle. (Alternatively, use a paper bag and snip off the tip.) Pipe small dots over the cleaned egg moulds and chill for 10 minutes. Spread the plain chocolate over the moulds, working fairly quickly so that the white chocolate does not smear into it. Finish as left, giving 1–2 more coats of the plain chocolate.

Latticed Eggs

Make as for Polka Dot Eggs, piping lines of white chocolate in opposite directions into the moulds.

Filigree Eggs

Complete the eggs as in the main recipe then drizzle or pipe melted chocolate in the same or contrasting colour over the eggs.

Nut Whirls

- 25 g/1 oz pistachio nuts, hazelnuts or broken walnuts
- 200 g/7 oz plain or milk chocolate, broken into pieces
- 25 g/1 oz unsalted butter

TO DECORATE:

- pistachio nuts, hazelnuts or broken walnuts
- crystallized fruit (optional)

1 If using pistachio nuts, soak them in boiling water for 1 minute, then peel away the skins.

2 Put 50 g/2 oz of the chocolate in a heatproof bowl over a saucepan of simmering water. Leave until melted.

3 Place small teaspoonfuls of the melted chocolate on a greaseproof paper-lined tray and spread to 2 cm/¾ inch rounds with the back of the spoon. Position a nut or piece of walnut on the centre of each.

4 Put the remaining chocolate in a bowl with the butter and melt over a saucepan of simmering water. Stir lightly and leave to cool until thickened enough to pipe.

5 Put the mixture in a piping bag fitted with a small star nozzle and pipe whirls on to the nuts to cover completely. Top each with a nut or crystallized fruit, if liked, and leave to set.

Makes about 30
Preparation time: 15 minutes

Chocolate Liqueur Cups

Paper sweet cases vary considerably in size. If possible, use the very small ones which are often coated in coloured foil.

CASES:

- 150 g/5 oz plain chocolate, broken into pieces

FILLING:

- 175 g/6 oz white chocolate, broken into pieces
- 4 tablespoons double cream
- 2 tablespoons brandy or rum

TO DECORATE:

- 50 g/2 oz plain chocolate, broken into pieces
- 25 g/1 oz white chocolate, broken into pieces
- small caraque or curls (see page 7) or edible gold leaf (optional)

1 Make the cases. Put the plain chocolate in a heatproof bowl over a saucepan of simmering water and leave until melted.
2 Spoon into 24 paper sweet cases, spreading up the sides with the back of a teaspoon. Invert on to a greaseproof paper-lined tray and chill until set.
3 Make the filling. Put the white chocolate in a bowl with the cream and leave over a saucepan of simmering water until melted. Stir in the brandy or rum. Leave until cool.
4 Spoon the liqueur cream into the cases until almost filled. Chill in the refrigerator until firm.

5 To decorate, melt the remaining plain and white chocolate as left, keeping them separate. Spoon the white chocolate into a piping bag fitted with a writing nozzle. (Alternatively, use a paper piping bag and snip off the merest tip.)
6 Spoon the plain chocolate over the filling to seal completely. While it is still runny, pipe a circle of white chocolate on to the plain and draw a cocktail stick through it to give a feathered effect. Alternatively, pipe lattice lines.
7 If using the caraque and gold leaf to decorate, position them before the chocolate has set.

Makes about 24
Preparation time: 45 minutes, plus chilling

VARIATION

Coffee Liqueur Cups

Use plain chocolate instead of white in the filling and omit the brandy or rum. Add 1 teaspoon of finely ground espresso, dissolved in 1 tablespoon boiling water with 2 tablespoons coffee-flavoured liqueur after melting. Decorate as left, or with chocolate-coated coffee beans.

Recipe Photographer:
Graham Kirk
Recipe Home Economist:
Joanna Farrow
Jacket Photographer:
Gus Filgate
Jacket Home Economist:
Louise Pickford